Z FOR ZEBRA

Reg Parsons

MINERVA PRESS

ATLANTA LONDON SYDNEY

Z FOR ZEBRA
Copyright © Reg Parsons 1999

ISBN 0 75410 744 2

First Published 1999 by
MINERVA PRESS
315–317 Regent Street
London W1R 7YB

Printed in Great Britain for Minerva Press

Z FOR ZEBRA

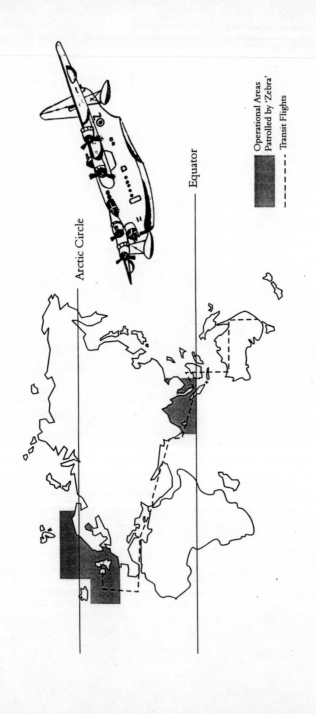

Arctic Circle

Equator

Operational Areas
Patrolled by 'Zebra'

----- Transit Flights

Dedicated to the crews
who flew the Boat over Burma with
such steadfast courage and determination

Introduction

Z for Zebra is an account of the Flight Engineer and the Air Gunners training experienced by a trainee Flight Engineer before joining a flying-boat operational squadron in World War Two, and the subsequent operational flying against German and Japanese submarines and shipping in areas as far apart as the North Atlantic above the Arctic circle where the crew were able to afford some protection to the convoys bound for Russia, but where they had to face the bitter cold and darkness of the long winter nights, and possible attacks by German aircraft.

Later the crew flew the aircraft out to join a squadron in Burma, where they carried out attacks against the shipping in the Gulf of Siam and the South China seas which was supplying the Japanese Imperial army then retreating back across Malaya and Burma, and where they were fortunate enough to fight off the too close attentions of a Japanese fighter bomber with no injury to the crew and little damage to the aircraft.

A detailed description of the big Sunderland flying-boat and its massive armament capability, is given in the first chapter, and its quite extraordinary versatility which enabled it to be deployed in such diverse roles as an efficient submarine killer, bomber, and passenger or freight carrier, becomes clear in subsequent chapters. The tactics used in all these roles, some of which were highly unconventional are fully described.

The crew were to witness at first hand the brutal savage

treatment meted out to their prisoners of war by the Japanese servicemen, and the depth of hatred felt by the prisoners and by the local population for the Japanese, which resulted in one instance of an indiscriminate massacre of Japanese officers in Dutch Borneo, in which the crew were also to take quite an innocent part.

About the Author

The author joined the Royal Air Force in January 1941, and after initial training at Blackpool was posted to a Flight Mechanics (engines) course at Locking. After successful completion of the course, he remained at Locking to take the Fitter IIE (engine) course, and trained on the engine with which he was to eventually fly, the nine cylinder radial Pegasus XVIII.

The next posting was to the flying-boat maintenance base at RAF Calshot, where he gained the experience on the Sunderland Mk.I, Walrus and the Shetland which was to stand him in good stead when the Air Gunners' course at Pembrey and the Flight Engineers' course at St Athan were completed and he joined a Sunderland crew.

Operational flying exercises to cover the convoys in the North Atlantic and the Russian convoys followed, and then a posting to join a squadron in Ceylon which soon moved into Burma as the Japanese armies were driven back. Offensive anti-shipping patrols were carried out over the Indian ocean, the Gulf of Siam and the South China Seas, resulting in the sinking of a number of strategic vessels supplying the Japanese Army.

After demobilisation, he spent a short period in various civilian jobs before rejoining the RAF in 1947, and then flying for the next twenty-four years as Flight Engineer on the Lincoln II, York CI, Washington B29, Shackleton Mk.I and Mk.II and for shorter periods on other four-engined aircraft. The last part of his service was spent as an Operations Room Controller.

After leaving the service in 1975, he became a professional woodcarver and teacher of woodcarving; and, despite advancing years, still teaches in the order of eighty students a year. In addition to teaching, he has regularly contributed articles to various woodworking magazines and has had books published on the techniques of woodcarving.

Glossary

astra dome	Perspex dome in the roof of the fuselage. Used to take sunshots
beaching legs	Substantial wheeled legs, used to bring a flying-boat up the slipway
the Burma Hump	The Chin Hills of central Burma
chine	The joint between the hull and the planing bottom
the deck	The ground
de-icer boots	Pulsating rubber boots, used for removing ice from the airframe
ditching	Crash landing in the sea
eight eighths	Dense cloud
G	Force of gravity
gate	Gate on the throttle quadrant to prevent overboosting the engine
gharry	Indian word for *lorry*, widely used in the RAF
IFF	A device that transmits a coded signal to identify the aircraft to friendly forces
intercostals	Ribs supporting the frame of a flying-boat
JU88	German fighter bomber
Mk.I eyeball	Term used for a visual search

ME109	German fighter
oggin	Term used by 'Boat Men' to describe water
pots	Engine cylinders
scow	Boat used to carry bombs or fuel
short slip	Stout rope looped at each end to enable the moorings to be quickly slipped
smoke float	Gives off smoke when dropped in the sea
step	The point where the planing bottom of a flying-boat steps, in order to break the suction on the hull
the stick	Aircraft's control column
tail-end Charlie	Tail Gunner
trots	Flying-boat moorings
VGO	Vickers Gas Operated machine-gun
Zero	Japanese fighter

Contents

Chapter One

Flight Engineer Training
at RAF St Athan

A light breeze gently ruffled the sunlit waters of the Solent, as the big flying-boat began to swing on her moorings when she felt the surge of power from the starting engines. The buoy moorings fell with a splash into the water, and a confused whirlpool of foam swirled under the port outer propeller as the captain opened up the outboard engine to turn her head out to sea and into wind.

She lay low in the water under a load of anti-submarine bombs, depth charges and two thousand gallons of high-octane aviation fuel; and yet the graceful lines of the white hull, and tall tail silhouetted cleanly against the green backdrop of the Isle of Wight, were unmistakable. For a short while, the propellers idled as the pre-take-off checks were carried out; and then there was a muffled roar which reverberated deafeningly off the great steel hangars at the top of the slipway, as the four Pegasus XVIII engines were opened up to take-off power. A bow wave started to curl away from under her bows as she slowly gathered speed, but with the pull of the suction under her hull, she seemed for a time reluctant to leave the water. Under the influence of a freshening wind, however, and a light pull back on the stick, she quickly came up on the step, with the keel now sending long, curving sheets of water out to each side as it sliced cleanly through the tips of the long swell rolling in from the English Channel.

A wave larger than the rest finally broke the suction on her hull, and with water streaming from the keel, she banked round in a graceful climbing curve which would bring her on to track, and then far out into the lonely Atlantic. There, her crew would have to face many hours of tedium, as they searched the apparently empty and limitless wastes of grey, heaving water for the deadly German submarines that were devastating our convoys at that time; and where they would also have to face possible attacks by JU88s or the more heavily armed Foke Wulfe Condor.

It was at that moment, standing on the slipway at Calshot, watching the graceful beauty of that great aircraft as it receded into the distance, that I decided to train on the Sunderland Flying-Boat when I started the Flight Engineers' course at RAF St Athan for which I had already been accepted. It was a decision that eventually took me halfway around the world, and into an area that saw possibly the worst and bloodiest fighting of World War Two.

The relentless driving rain and low, grey mist that covered the Welsh hills could not dampen the rising excitement that I felt as I walked through the great steel doors of one of St Athan's Hangars, for the start of the course. The vast floor area was dominated by three aircraft. In the centre and in one corner, stood a Stirling and a Lancaster bomber, their stark, black, menacing outlines contrasting sharply with the white, shapely hull of the big Sunderland Flying-Boat that stood on its massive beaching legs in the other corner.

By the side of each aircraft was a sectioned engine: a Bristol Pegasus XVIII in the case of the Sunderland. There was also a small huddle of chairs and a blackboard, the limit of the training aids available to us as simulators were, as yet, unheard of in those days. All the ground- and air-training was carried out 'hands on'. This did not leave much room for mistakes, as many unfortunate crews found to their cost when they were eventually crewed up and started their training. Heavy Conversion Unit flying could be nearly as hazardous as 'Ops.', and it was where, sadly, many new crews came to grief, partly due to their inexperience.

A flight of wooden steps led up to the bow door on the port side of the aircraft. This was the door normally used for access from a dinghy, as it was only a short distance above the water line, unlike the starboard aft door which was some considerable height above the water.

Stowed in the bow compartment was all the equipment required for anchoring or mooring the aircraft: the anchor and winch, boat hook, and the short slip. The short slip was a short length of stout rope with loops spliced in each end. It was used to enable the moorings to be quickly released once the engines were started by slipping one of the loops off the bollard, on a signal from the pilot, and allowing it to slide free through the wire hawser on top of the mooring buoy. Right up in the nose was a bollard that could be erected and secured to the nose, once the front turret had been wound back on its rails, out of the way to enable the mooring to be carried out.

The Frazer Nash gun turret contained two Vickers gas operated .303 machine guns, which had a much slower rate of fire than the Brownings fitted to the majority of the aircraft's gun turrets. But they did have the advantage over the Brownings, that if an ammunition pan jammed it was a simple matter, taking only seconds, to unclip the old pan from the top of the breech block and replace it with a new one, and then recock the gun. The Browning, on the other hand, with its long, vulnerable lines of rounds in racks stretching back well behind the turret, was often subject to jamming, which could take some time to free, quite possibly making the difference between life and death, when under attack.

On later Mks. of Sunderland, the nose twin gun turret was supplemented by four fixed Brownings fired by the pilot, who had to aim the aircraft at the target, quite often when he was at wave-top height, which required flying skills of a very high order. The combined effect of six thousand rounds a minute pouring into a target from the bow guns, was dramatic. It was usually sufficient to completely disable a small coaster, without the need to use the bombs or depth charges hanging in the bomb bay. They could be saved for larger targets.

To the right of the bow door, on the starboard side, was a toilet compartment, a very unusual luxury on a military aircraft. It was a leftover from the old Imperial Airways C-Class flying-boats, when passengers had to be accommodated in the utmost comfort. Also, in the bow compartment, was a flight of aluminium steps, which were the main access up to the flight deck.

The next compartment aft on the lower deck was the wardroom, which contained a central removable table with a canvas bunk situated on each side; where meals could be eaten in reasonable comfort, and a comfortable night's sleep obtained on the many occasions when it was necessary to spend the night on the aircraft.

Immediately aft of the wardroom was the galley, which contained a sink, two Primus stoves for cooking, and various cupboards for food storage. Quite good meals could be prepared and cooked there, but the culinary delights that usually appeared on the flight deck, often smelling of cordite fumes, gun oil, and paraffin, were rarely up to Imperial Airways standards. It came as no surprise to me that the big, grey water rat who decided to join us one dark night on the river Pegu in Burma and who flew with us out in the darkness of the wing for some hundreds of hours would quite often refuse to eat our leftover flight rations. It much preferred a freshly opened tin of stew, or perhaps, more surprisingly, the plastic knobs on top of the throttle levers. These he would chew enthusiastically in the dead of night when nobody was about, eventually leaving us with four mangled knobs with which to operate the throttles. But more of that later.

On each side of the galley were two hatches through which drogues could be deployed at a signal from the pilot as he approached a buoy. The drogues would fill with water, creating a great deal of drag, slowing the aircraft up to a walking pace. This gave the pilot much more control over the aircraft if he was going too fast, although if the buoy was missed by the gunner in the bows at the first attempt, which was not an uncommon experience, particularly in bad weather, it was then almost impossible to trip the water out of the drogues whilst the aircraft was still moving. This then meant a very slow and laborious round trip to come up on the buoy again, whilst still dragging the water-filled drogues along beside the aircraft. This was an event that always afforded considerable amusement to any onlookers who were not directly involved.

Also mounted adjacent to the galley hatches were two Vickers gas-operated .303 machine guns, similar to those fitted in the front turret. Unlike those, however, they were free-mounted. The galley guns were seldom used, as all the available gunners were deployed on guns that were generally in a more advantageous position. Although, on several occasions, the crewman cooking a meal in the galley would drop what he was doing and blast off a few rounds from the galley guns when we unexpectedly discovered a small coaster or sampan concealed under the lee of one of the tropical islands that cover the inshore waters of the Gulf of Siam.

The bomb bay, which was situated between the wings, was the next compartment aft from the galley. The bomb racks were secured to trolleys which ran on rails in the roof of the bomb bay; these trolleys could be hand cranked out along the underside of the wings to their dropping position, after first, manually, opening two large doors on each side of the hull. On later Mks. of Sunderland, the doors could be opened, and the bomb racks deployed, by pulling up a large lever situated by the side of the first pilot.

The bomb doors would open with a violent crash, propelled downwards by strong lengths of bungee rubber. The bomb trolleys would then trundle unsteadily out on their rails to their allotted position on the underside of the wings. The whole system appeared to be very Heath Robinson at first sight, and brought a derisory grin to the faces of the Bomber Command flight engineers, who were training on their very smart, brand new, Lancasters and Stirlings. But we found the system to be reliable, and it worked very well in practice. There was, of course, a slight delay between the bomb doors being selected open and the bombs being ready to drop; which could make all the difference between a kill or a near miss, if a submarine suddenly surfaced in front of the aircraft. But this was a very unlikely eventuality, and the slight delay certainly never affected us in any of the attacks that we were to carry out against shipping in the South China Seas.

The retractable bomb racks did have the considerable advantage that they could be reloaded in the air if necessary, with the smaller types of ordinance, such as smoke- or flame-floats. Although we never found this practice to be necessary.

A UK-based Australian squadron regularly rearmed their bomb racks in the air. They also fitted a five hundred gallon fuel tank on the floor of the bomb bay, in order to increase their range or endurance. This must have made it all a bit crowded in there, and a little hazardous too, with the Primuses blazing merrily away in the next compartment.

Also in the bomb bay were two fuel jettison pipes which could be extended to below the bottom of the hull. This enabled any jettisoned fuel to clear the aircraft well away from the red hot engine exhaust rings.

The final rear compartment aft of the bomb bay contained the main armament, which consisted, on the later Mks., of a two gun mid-upper turret, a free-mounted, massively powerful, .5 machine gun situated at each of the port and starboard hatches, and, right at the end of the tail, a four-gun turret. There was also a cradle for safely storing pyrotechnics, such as flame- and smoke-floats adjacent to the manually operated flare chute; and there was also a position for the vertical camera and the rails which carried the long lines of .303 ammunition for the tail turrets' four Brownings which could not be accommodated in the turret for lack of room.

A small bench with a vice, which was fitted on the port side of the rear compartment, was useful for any maintenance work that had to be carried out when the crew was operating alone and away from base; which the squadron aircraft in the Far East often had to do, sometimes for weeks on end.

This very heavy concentration of fire-power made the Sunderland a very formidable adversary, and led the German Air Force pilots to name it 'Stachelschwein', or 'The Flying Porcupine', as they were often on the very lethal receiving end of it, much to their obvious discomfiture.

The flight-deck, which was reached either by a ladder in the bow compartment or a ladder in the rear compartment, contained positions for the two pilots, flight engineer, navigator, and the radar and radio operators. It was particularly spacious compared with today's aircraft, with plenty of room to move around, which was a valuable asset on the long, often boring flights over the sea.

Just forward of the pilot's windscreen, and situated in the roof of the bow compartment, were two small flaps which could be opened from inside the aircraft. It was difficult, although quite possible, even when airborne, to put a hand through the opening and wipe the windscreen clean. It was, of course, a sensible and very useful facility, as salt spray would often obscure the windscreen during rough weather conditions. But it did give the crew a lot of amusement to watch the faces of unsuspecting passengers, when they saw a hand appear in front of them apparently from outer space; and we never missed an opportunity to try it out on any passenger who asked for a look round the flight-deck.

In the roof of the flight-deck was a perspex astra dome through which the navigator took his sunshots. It also had an escape hatch through which access could be gained to the wings. In the event of a ditching, two ten-man rubber dinghies were automatically deployed from the top surface of the wings if the flying-boat sank.

Situated in the leading edges of the wings, and on each side of the Pegasus XVIII engines that were fitted to the early Mks. of Sunderland, were maintenance platforms, which could be lowered in order to carry out work on the engines. The starboard inboard engine platform also provided access to the auxiliary power unit which could be used to both provide electrical power to the aircraft, when the engines were shut down, and a rather ineffective pump for pumping out wet bilges. Despite all its defects, the pump that was fitted to our first 'Zebra', undoubtedly saved our aircraft from sinking one stormy night off the Scottish coast; and it also probably saved all our lives, by preventing the water level reaching the already primed depth charges hanging in the bomb bay.

The availability of electrical power when at anchor on

the water, and the vast roominess of the interior of the hull, meant that the Sunderland could be deployed for considerable periods away from base, with the aircraft being used to house the crew in reasonable comfort.

A certain amount of limited maintenance work could also be carried out on her, although work required on the exterior of the hull often meant the construction of a raft. This we had to do on more than one occasion, using anything that was locally available, some coconut tree trunks lashed together and a few empty fifty gallon oil drums; with the predictable result that we were regularly deposited in the water from the unstable platform, often losing any equipment that was not securely tied on in the process.

In the offensive anti-submarine, or anti-shipping role, the Sunderland usually carried four two hundred and fifty pound anti-submarine bombs, and four two hundred and fifty pound depth charges, which, coupled with the sixteen machines guns that she carried, made her a deadly adversary for an enemy ship or submarine.

Her comparatively slow range speed, compared with other aircraft of the time, about one hundred and thirty-five knots, was no disadvantage in her maritime role. Indeed, the slow speed was often an advantage when investigating a radar contact. The craft was able to orbit slowly over a small patch of sea, in order to investigate the swirl from a possible crash-diving submarine, or perhaps seek a hapless survivor from a shot down aircraft.

In the event of a fighter attack, however, over two hundred knots could be achieved; which, coupled with an extraordinary manoeuvrability in the air, made her an excellent fighting machine. We were to be very grateful for this later on.

The depth charges were primarily intended to be used as an anti-submarine weapon. A depth charge would be dropped on each side of the submarine. The resulting crushing blast, as they exploded, would cause the collapse of the submarine's pressure hull.

When we were carrying out anti-shipping operations in the Gulf of Siam, operational experience quickly taught us that depth charges were just as effective when used in this way against small coasters. This knowledge enabled us to deny the Japanese army some badly needed supplies during their retreat across Malaya by sinking a coaster, and a sampan that it was towing, with depth charges. We also discovered, quite by accident, that our two hundred knots would enable us to skip-bomb moored targets, that were impossible to bomb from above, due usually to overhanging cliffs.

On one occasion on an anti-shipping patrol, when our bomb bay was empty and there was only sufficient ammunition left in the guns to fight off a possible fighter attack on our return to base, we flew over a large junk carrying strategic supplies at mast top height. Using all our available power, we gave the crew a fright and possibly deterred them from future runs.

To our surprise, the sails of the junk filled with the blast from the four slipstreams, causing it to keel right over until the sails were level with the surface of the water. When the junk had slowly righted herself, the military vehicle that had been lashed near the stern broke away, and disappeared over the side. It was very probable that a certain amount of damage had also been caused inside the vessel. On future sorties, we were able to obtain some limited results against sailing ships, when on the way back to base at the end of a sortie, even when all our bombs and depth charges had been exhausted.

With all her armaments removed, the vast size of the Sunderland's hull meant that she could also be used as a very effective passenger and freight carrying aircraft.

Immediately after the end of the Far East war, quite apart from their other commitments, the Sunderland flying-boat squadrons carried forty ex-prisoners of war at a time from Singapore to India, on the first leg of their way home to England and Holland; and during the same period, over one thousand women and children were evacuated from Batavia. Also, many of the starving peoples of North Malaya were rescued from starvation by the Sunderlands who were able to lift ten thousand pounds of rice at a time in their bomb bay for delivery to the port of Quantan; where, incidentally, the hazards of taking off and landing, without the help of a control launch to monitor the area for floating debris, was dramatically demonstrated when one of the squadron's aircraft hit either a log, or possibly a large sea crocodile on landing, and had its planing bottom ripped out. Fortunately, there was no serious injury to either the crew or passengers on board.

This transport facility was made very good use of in Burma, when Sunderlands were used to ferry in arms and medical supplies to General Wingate's force, and then bring out his wounded from many hundreds of miles behind the enemy lines. They had to thread their way through the often cloud-covered peaks of the mountains of central Burma, and land on isolated lakes and rivers in the interior. It was an operation that could not have been carried out by any other type of aircraft in those days, which was well before the advent of the helicopter.

In one extreme case, eighty-seven people were on board one aircraft when it was used to evacuate army personnel from Crete, under the noses of the German forces; although there is some doubt as to whether it was actually able to get airborne, or whether it was just taxied back to base on the water.

The ability of the Sunderland flying-boat to so effectively and reliably carry out the very wide variety of roles that were assigned to it, many of which it had not been designed for, made it probably the most versatile aircraft ever flown by the Royal Air Force; and no aircraft that has been produced since has been able to match its stalwart versatility, or the lasting loyalty that it always engendered in its crews.

Despite the limited facilities available to us, and the comparatively short duration of the course, a great deal of valuable information was packed into the three months' Flight Engineers' course at St Athan. It was to prove particularly valuable in the Far East, where we often operated alone and far from base for very considerable periods, without the benefit of servicing crews.

I also thought it wise, under the circumstances, to take the opportunity to learn to swim. This undoubtedly saved my bacon on more than one occasion when I was unceremoniously deposited in the water from a wet, slippery and bouncing wing.

I left RAF St Athan loaded down with flying gear, which included the uncomfortable, electrically heated Sidcot flying suit, ideal for the draughty high-altitude bomber aircraft crews who often flew in temperatures of thirty or forty degrees below freezing, but of little value for low-level maritime flying. A leather helmet fitted with goggles, in case a wind screen was shot out, silk gloves inside leather gauntlets, and calf length sheepskin flying boots, completed the flying kit.

Although the Flight Engineers' course had now been completed successfully, the coveted Flight Engineers' Brevet would have to wait until the Air Gunners' course had been completed and passed at RAF Pembrey, also in South Wales. Unlike Bomber Command Flight Engineers, it was necessary for all the 'Boat' men to double up as air gunners; which, incidentally, also helped to reduce the tedium of long operational flights over the sea. This was a duty also shared by other members of a 'Boat' crew who could often only be restrained with difficulty from blasting a few rounds off at the 'Oggin', when there was nothing else to do and boredom set in during long all-night winter patrols over the North Atlantic. We were quickly to find out, though, when we did eventually arrive in the Far East, that boredom was going to be the least of the problems that was going to afflict us from then on.

Chapter Two

Air Gunners' Training
at RAF Pembrey

Our first introduction to the course at Pembrey was a short lecture on discipline by the station warrant officer, who had a distinct aversion to any airman with hair more than a quarter of an inch long, and a commanding voice that could shatter a pint pot at one hundred yards. For all that, he was a thoroughly decent man who would wait patiently every night, and in all weathers, at the railway station halt, in order to escort the young and vulnerable WAAFs safely back to their billets. It was a self-imposed duty, but a very necessary one, as the bromide that it was rumoured laced our tea in order to subdue the young airmen's more romantic notions, always seemed to be singularly ineffective, as far as I could judge; but, in retrospect, I am not sure that all the young WAAFs fully appreciated his concern, to judge from the occasional outcome.

The ground lectures were given in wooden huts, which were warmed by the ubiquitous service coal stove; a very pleasant change from the great hangar at St Athan where it had been necessary to huddle up in our great coats in order to keep out the cold, and damp, of a Welsh winter.

Aircraft and ship recognition were of the greatest importance, as both friendly and enemy aircraft could look very similar when seen in silhouette against a bright sky, and there was never time to make a leisurely assessment of the situation when a fighter appeared from out of the sun.

In addition to the necessary ability to be able to determine whether an aircraft was friendly or not, the length of a fighter's wing-span was used by the gunner to determine the range of the target. For example, if the length of an aircraft's wing-span was known, and it filled the red ring of the gunner's gunsight, the range could then be fairly accurately estimated by the gunner. This saved him uselessly blasting off a few rounds too early, when the target was still well out of range, and, therefore, wasting valuable ammunition that might very well be required later on in the sortie to ward off another attack. Opening fire much too early was very easy to do under the pressure and excitement of the moment, as I can readily confirm.

The rules of sighting, which also formed an important part of the Air Gunner's course, were surprisingly complex; and although they were fairly simple to understand, when being explained in the quiet and security of the lecture room, they were very difficult to remember when the gunner had become disorientated by tight high G-turns in the air, and the target appeared to be moving through his gun sight in all directions, whilst violent evasive action was being carried out by the pilot.

Practice ground firing was carried out from hydraulically operated twin-gun turrets on the firing range, against simulated aircraft moving targets. The noise from the twin machine-guns in the confined space of the turret, with the twin breech blocks only inches from the gunner's head, was shattering. Even when wearing a leather flying-helmet, the cordite fumes that filled the turret caught the back of the throat. But it was an exciting change to the continuous lectures that we had had to endure up to this point.

The ground lectures slowly became interspersed with flying details which were flown in Ansons, with Martinets being used to either tow target drogues, or as simulated fighter-attack aircraft. The occasional Spitfire or Hurricane was also used for this purpose, when one could be spared from the fighting, which made the whole exercise much more realistic. It also gave the fighter pilot a chance to keep his hand in, in preparation for a return to the air battles then taking place over Southern Britain.

The Anson was fitted with a Browning mid-upper twin-gun turret, which had a seat very much like a bicycle saddle. The seat was elevated and depressed hydraulically at the same time as the guns by operating a twist grip on the control arm. This arrangement kept the gunner in line with his gun-sight, but unfortunately for the poor gunner, when the turret was vacated and left to its own devices, the hydraulics would creep, which would in turn depress the guns and raise the saddle. The only way in which the turret could then be entered, was to reach up from underneath, with considerable difficulty, turn the twist grip in order to lower the seat, and then leap into the turret like a scalded cat before you became impaled by the rising seat. The part of the body most likely to be affected by this procedure was regarded by most young airmen as being of the utmost importance, so the acrobatics that were performed, whilst getting into the turret, were well worth watching.

The day that I trudged for the first time, in heavy flying-boots, across the sparkling frost-covered grass to the aircraft, and climbed into the old Anson to get airborne for the first time, was probably the most exciting day of my life. It was also the day that I made my first mistake, because I unknowingly allowed the plug on the end of my intercom lead to dangle in the long wet grass, with the result that when it was plugged in there was a high-pitched howling noise on the intercom that made speech impossible. The pilot who had been afflicted by trainee gunners in the same way a hundred times before, made his disapproval very clear, and I certainly did not make the same mistake again.

Immediately after take-off, the gunner's first duty was to wind up the undercarriage, which on the early Mks. of the Anson was manually operated and took in excess of one hundred laborious turns before the red undercarriage warning lights went out. Then came the trick of climbing into the turret, without being left with a high pitched voice. If all this was achieved without incident, there was time to settle back for a short while as the aircraft continued its leisurely climb up to the exercise altitude.

Although we were still in mid winter, it being the early part of February, the weather was perfect for flying, with each morning producing a crisp sharp frost and a lovely clear blue sky.

On many occasions since, when spending long, boring hours flying over endless vistas of brown featureless desert, or the unending dark green of the jungle canopy, I have longed for the sight of the brilliant greens of the Welsh countryside, the dark purples and browns of the mountains, and the distant shimmering silver-grey of the sea, that I could see from my turret on those lovely, early winter mornings.

The airborne exercises consisted mainly of two types. Live gun firing into a drogue, which was towed by a Martinet, and cine-gun exercises, against simulated attacks by fighter aircraft. Each round that we fired was tipped with a different coloured paint, a different colour for each of the two trainee gunners that were carried on each sortie. This enabled the drogues to be checked at the end of each exercise, and the correct number of hits allocated to each gunner.

I found this to be particularly humiliating, because although I was confident when airborne that my long lines of tracer fire were consistently hitting the drogue, my average number of hits for the course was only about three per cent. Although I must say that I don't think that anybody else did very much better than that.

The low number of hits was partly accounted for by the cone of fire produced by the vibrating guns, which amounted to about fifty feet at twelve hundred yards, so a much greater number of hits would have been recorded on a larger target such as an aircraft. Well, that's my story anyway.

Although the live gun firing was very valuable practice and had a deadly serious purpose, it was also great fun. But it did not provide the sheer thrill and excitement generated by the simulated fighter attacks. The fighter pilots, who were mostly old hands from the Battle of Britain, knew every trick in the book, and quite a few more, and they threw everything that they could at us.

The main form of attack that was carried out by most fighters was the 'Curve of Pursuit'. In this form of attack, the fighter pilot would position his aircraft on the beam of the target aircraft and about one thousand feet above, preferably with the sun behind him in order to blind the gunners. He would then turn in towards the target to bring his fixed, forward-looking guns to bear, and then make a second turn in order to compensate for the target's forward movement.

It was at this point that the fighter would come within the twelve hundred yard range of the target's guns, and both aircraft would open fire. To limit the time of the engagement, the target aircraft would then turn and climb into the attack. The very high G-forces imposed upon the fighter pilot, as he attempted to follow the target aircraft round in the tight turn, whilst keeping his guns bearing on the target, would often force him to either break off the attack, or blackout.

Anyway, that was the theory; although, in my rather unhappy experience, it did not always quite work out like that because it was only some low, dense cloud drifting off the coast of Car Nicobar near the Andaman Islands, into which we providentially climbed, that saved us from the too close attentions of a Japanese fighter bomber. The enemy carried out a classic, textbook 'Curve of Pursuit' attack, and then grimly followed us through the climbing turn, without obviously knowing anything about the blacking-out bit. We were jolly lucky to get away that day with only a few holes punched in the hull well above the water-line, and no serious injury to the crew. But more of that later.

Because the flying-boat normally operated at about one thousand feet above the sea, its more normal means of defence against the 'Curve of Pursuit' was to descend as close to the sea as possible, which for a 'Boat' crew, used to spending long hours at low level, was very close indeed.

This tactic ensured that the fighter was compelled to stay above the target, where all the flying-boat's guns could be brought to bear in defence. It was a particularly brave man who would press home an attack in those circumstances. And of those with enough nerve to try it, few lived to tell the tale.

This form of defence was well suited to the 'Boat' crews, as it would only take seconds to drop down to sea-level when the heart-stopping call for 'Action Stations, Action Stations' came over the intercom.

There were a few isolated instances over the North Atlantic where German JU88 crews attempted to use the flying-boats' low-level defence to their advantage, by attempting to bomb the aircraft from above. But there are no known instances of this form of attack being successful, because big as she was, the Sunderland could be cranked round really hard, and turned on the proverbial sixpence when necessary; and practising evasive action against fighters was also a very important part of a 'Boat' man's training.

An alternative form of fighter attack was from the front. This attack was only very rarely used, because the closing speed of the two aircraft would be in the region of five hundred miles an hour. The time in which the target would be within range of the fighter's guns, therefore, was very limited. The fighter also became a target for the flying-boat's beam guns and tail turret as he banked away.

This position was reversed when flying through mountain ranges, because the fighter could spring a surprise attack by appearing above the brow of a hill where he had been orbiting ready to spring the trap, or around the side of a mountain. It was always a particularly heart-stopping moment when, during training, a Spitfire would appear, apparently from out of nowhere, in front of the bows; and it always seemed an eternity before the gunner recovered from the surprise and shock and was able to depress the gun triggers in order to activate the cine cameras. Although, in reality, it would probably only have been a fraction of a second.

Although the frontal attack was rarely used, it was one that we always had to be very much aware of, as the offensive anti-shipping operations that we were to eventually carry out in the Gulf of Siam and the South China Seas always entailed a high-level transit across the hills of central Siam. Because of the limited power of the engines at altitude, it was often necessary to thread our way through the mountain peaks, which left us very open and vulnerable to a frontal attack.

Fortunately for us, the fighter always relied on being vectored by ground radar in order to spring this type of attack, and Japanese radar cover over Siam was very limited in those days – to which we had contributed a small part, by blasting away a radar station that we had inadvertently flown across on our way to the Gulf.

Apart from the German fighters and JU88s, whose operations were confined by their limited range, the only other aircraft that presented a danger to the Sunderland in the North Atlantic and the Bay of Biscay, was the four-engined Focke Wulfe Condor. This was a well-armed aircraft that was often used by the Germans to monitor the movement of British convoys, and then to pass the information on to their U-boat packs. This activity occasionally brought them into conflict with the crews of the Sunderland, who would be well aware that a Condor might be cruising in the vicinity of a convoy, and would be keeping a very sharp look out for them.

A stand-up fight would often ensue when they did meet, with both aircraft flying wing-tip, to wing-tip, and blasting away at each other rather like two ancient galleons. The Sunderland, however, was very much more heavily armed and manoeuvrable, so it always had the advantage over the Focke Wulfe Condor.

I was sorry to leave Pembrey because, although the course had been intense, it had been both interesting and, to one new to flying, very exciting. This was particularly true of the trips that I managed to scrounge, on my days off, in the twin-seat Martinets when they were acting in their fighter role.

Although I must say that the sorties did not do a great deal for my digestion,

that was something all coastal crews had to quickly get used to. Even a big flying-boat, when flying at low-level in a mid winter North Atlantic storm, or through a tropical hurricane, could get tossed about like a feather.

Anyhow, I now wore the coveted Flight Engineer's brevet, and the next step was to meet the crew with whom I was to spend the next two years, and to finally start the flying part of the course on the Sunderland at No. 4 (C) Operational Conversion Unit, at Invergordan on the Moray Firth, Scotland.

Chapter Three

Heavy Conversion Unit Training at RAF Invergordan

Winter had given away to a reluctant spring in the highlands, and there was still a deep layer of snow covering the higher peaks of the Scottish mountains. The turbulent waters of the Moray Firth were a steely grey, which reflected the leaden sky, and a bitterly cold northerly wind blew the early morning frost from the massed ranks of pine trees which were growing on the hillside, leading down to the water's edge. But there riding high on the foam-flecked water, with all the graceful beauty of a flock of white swans that had been lined up by the wind and tide, were moored the Sunderlands on which we were to train.

A small power-dinghy scurried busily around the trots of moored flying-boats, carrying maintenance crews to the aircraft; and a high speed control launch, with a mass of white water boiling from her stern, curved swiftly away from the jetty to meet a returning flying-boat whose engines could just be heard in the distance.

The aircraft made a leisurely circuit of the area, and then turned into wind for the final approach. The captain held the aircraft just above the surface of the water for a short time, and then allowed her to slowly descend, until the tip of the keel was slicing keenly through the wave-tops. The noise from her engines suddenly died as the power was cut and she settled down gently into the water in a wild swirling mass of foam. Her control launch, now looking tiny against the Sunderland's massive hull, followed her closely in as she taxied in between the trots, and, against the tide, up to the buoy. The front turret was wound back, and the gunner in the bows passed the short slip through the loop on the top of the buoy, and quickly secured it to the bollard as the engines subsided into silence.

Another long, twelve hour all-night patrol through the bitter cold of the North Atlantic was over, and the tired crew could at last get some sleep. In all the subsequent hours that I spent on the 'Boat', I never failed to thrill at the sight of those great aircraft landing and taking off. It was a dramatic spectacle that could never be matched by land-based aircraft whose streamlined shape is always spoilt by their ugly undercarriages when on the deck.

To add to the many hours of instruction at both St Athan and St Mawgan, still more ground lectures now followed; although, in addition to the usual aircraft and ship recognition, seamanship now became an important and interesting part of the curriculum.

Great stress was laid on mooring-up, as it was very much an acquired skill, and it could be both difficult and very dangerous in high seas and gale force winds. But it was a skill that the whole crew had to master, because under operational conditions it was quite possible that not all the crew would be available at the end of a sortie to carry out the mooring-up duties.

I quickly discovered, after the first few rather abortive attempts, that the flight engineer was always much too busy to spare the time, when the slipping or mooring-up of the aircraft was required. The straight gunners, as they were then called, were elected for that particular pleasure.

We now formed up into the crews with whom we would be flying on the squadrons, by mixing together in one of the large hangars, and there deciding which crew to join up with. It was a good system. It allowed old comrades to serve on the same crew. But it was quite impossible, at that stage, to be able to judge who was likely to be the most skilled pilot or navigator, or which of the gunners would be able to hold their nerve long enough with a German ME109 or Japanese Zero on the tail. But, in the event, I made a good choice, and the ten-man crew that I joined up with worked well and efficiently together, often under the most trying and difficult circumstances, for the two years that followed. This was largely due to the influence of the Captain, who although a quiet and unfailingly courteous man, nevertheless commanded the respect and loyalty of the whole crew; and on at least one occasion, was responsible for saving all our lives by his outstanding skill and personal courage.

The crew consisted of the Captain, who had just completed a tour in the Far East as a Co-Pilot on a Sunderland squadron, so he was already a very experienced pilot, and a Canadian Co-Pilot who was fresh out of flying training but very steady and quick to learn.

Immediately behind the pilots was the position for the navigator. He had to navigate by dead reckoning quite often for fifteen hours or more at a time over the sea, with only very little help from a hand-held sextant when the sun occasionally obliged by showing its face. Not very often in the middle of the winter over the North Atlantic.

The primitive radar could also be used to give a rough fix when coasting in, although its range was very limited; and yet, despite the limitations of his equipment, our navigator consistently arrived on task, or back at base, with only the error of a few miles either way. This gave the crew a great deal of confidence in his abilities when we were nervously threading our way through the cloud-covered peaks of the Chin Hills in central Burma, which we were called upon to do on a number of occasions, or when we arrived back at base, with the cloud down on the deck.

It was not uncommon for us to receive a request from a Royal Navy warship for an accurate position, particularly over the North Atlantic, where in the winter the Navy's ships would quite often not get a sight of the sun or the stars for days on end. Such was the high reputation for accuracy, quite rightly earned, by our navigators.

Behind the Navigator's position, on the flight deck, was the Flight Engineer's panel, which was continuously manned by one of the two Flight Engineers on board, the other engineer manning the bow gun turret for that shift. On the other side of the flight deck were the positions for the Radar and WT Operators. These positions were manned by two Wireless Operators, and a Wireless Operator Mechanic or WOM who, with the greatest expertise, was able to get the best possible results from his antiquated equipment; and through some extraordinary magic, only known to himself, enabled the crew to hear, through his earphones, during one black night on the Pegu River in Burma, the startling and completely unexpected news that Germany had surrendered.

The three Wireless Operators also took it in turns to man one of the heavy beam .5 machine-guns, and, just as importantly, when they could be spared from their other duties, they took it in turns to prepare the meals in the galley, which could often be a difficult job with the aircraft bouncing round the sky in a monsoon storm.

The four-gun tail turret, and the other .5 beam machine-gun, were manned by two so-called Straight Gunners. They also normally dealt with the mooring-up, although any of the other crew members could also be called upon to carry out that duty.

The Straight Gunners were two taciturn Scots, who were both dead shots and proved to be utterly reliable under fire; and yet, despite the inevitable hardness that followed the dreadful and harrowing scenes that we were to witness and take part in during our tour in the Far East, they both treated the exhausted and emaciated ex-prisoners of war that we eventually flew back from Singapore to India with a tender kindness, and a depth of understanding, that seemed surprising coming from two such apparently hardened men.

The first few flying exercises on any course in those days, tended to be hazardous, with the aircraft being handled by inexperienced crew members, who had not had the benefit of a simulator to first iron out the wrinkles. So, for safety, the first few flying exercises where carried out with just the flight deck crew on board, accompanied, in our case, by an Australian screen crew who had already had a good deal of experience of operational flying.

The exercises consisted mainly of aircraft familiarisation and circuits, which could be more accurately described as circuits and ricochets. But the pilots quickly got the hang of the landings and take-offs; and the extreme accuracy and skill that was required to taxi a big flying-boat up to a buoy, in all the varying weather conditions that the early Scottish spring could throw at them.

Practice stalling was also carried out during this phase of the course. It was not nearly as hairy as it now sounds, as the Sunderland had few vices, and there was plenty of warning of the incipient stall from the shaking tail plane and control column as the turbulence from the stalling wings caught her. She would also stall cleanly straight ahead when the power was pulled off, with a quick recovery and very little tendency to drop a wing, once the throttles were banged open and the speed allowed to build up.

Stalling was certainly easy enough to carry out in practice, but not nearly as much fun when the stall was involuntary, and in a force ten gale, as we were to find out later.

To carry out the stall, the flying-boat was climbed to about seven thousand feet and into a clear patch of sky. The area was closely checked for other aircraft. Then, once she was trimmed straight and level, all the power was pulled off, and the control column moved steadily back to maintain height while the speed dropped off.

At about eighty knots, the tail and control column would begin to shake and the nose would suddenly drop, leaving anything not lashed down suspended in mid-air. The power was then immediately restored, and the speed allowed to build up. She would quickly recover, probably losing less than a thousand feet during the recovery.

After the initial familiarisation exercises, when it was judged by the screen crew that we were by now a little less likely to write ourselves off, we were joined, rather uneasily, by the rest of the crew.

The first few sorties consisted mainly of air-to-air gunnery firing, in order to help us give a good account of ourselves if we did get jumped by a fighter whilst on the course. This was followed by practice anti-submarine bomb attacks on simulated targets.

The targets were towed behind high-speed launches at about the speed of a submarine transiting on the surface. The aim was to drop a practice bomb, one on each side of the target. In an actual attack against a hostile submarine, the resulting crushing blast of the two exploding depth-charges would cause the submarine's pressure hull to collapse – normally a pretty terminal result.

The initial training was then followed by operational flying exercises, which consisted of actual convoy support flying. This was despite the fact that we were still under training, and not fully worked up as an operational crew.

The use of inexperienced crews in the convoy support role was vitally necessary at that time, because of the pressure to get as many aircraft out on task as possible, and in order to afford some protection to the convoys crossing the North Atlantic. Convoys were then under constant attack from German submarine packs.

Although we were never used in the convoy close support role, we did, however, spend many hours carrying out distant support. This normally involved flying an in-line patrol, during which parallel tracks were flown about five miles apart, and approximately thirty or forty miles ahead of the convoy's track. This was often a good place to catch an unsuspecting U-boat on the surface, charging his depleted batteries before diving in readiness for an attack on the convoy.

During all the operational flying that we did on the course, we were never fortunate enough to actually spot a U-boat on the surface. On many occasions, however, we were diverted from track to investigate either a radar contact or a suspicious swirl on the surface of the sea. These usually turned out to be either an innocent school of porpoises or the wreckage from a previously torpedoed freighter.

But on the odd occasion, there was nothing that could be positively identified when we arrived over the area, so the swirl could possibly have been the disturbance from a crash-diving submarine. In such a case, the time spent on patrol would not have been wasted if, we had kept our underwater friends bottled up, and using more of their already depleted batteries so preventing them from carrying out their attack on the convoy.

The day eventually came when we were judged to be a reasonably efficient, if inexperienced, maritime crew. We were then detailed to carry out the next operational flying exercise solo, without the support and advice of the screen crew. This exercise again turned out to be a convoy distant support patrol in the North Atlantic.

It was a particularly exciting moment for me when I climbed from the dinghy into the bow of the big flying-boat as a fully fledged Flight Engineer. After all the long months of intensive training, I was in charge of my own boat at last.

The rest of the crew quickly followed me in, and clanked noisily in their heavy flying-boots across the metal decking to their various crew positions, where they plugged into the intercom, and briefly checked in one by one. From then on the only messages that would be passed over the intercom would be short, terse commands in case the intercom was suddenly required for an emergency call, to report a fighter attack or a possible submarine sighting.

The whining noise of the gun turrets being checked as they were revolved, with the guns being elevated and depressed, and the clanking of the anchor chain as it was winched in, in readiness to slip the moorings, and the general hum of background noise as the crew went about their equipment checks, faded quickly into the background, as the airframe began to shake and vibrate when the outboard engines coughed noisily into life. As soon as they had settled down, with temperatures and pressures normal, the moorings were slipped, and we taxied out through the two trots of moored Sunderlands to our take-off position into wind. Each pair of engines were taken up to full power for a quick check, and then with clearance from our control launch, the four throttles were pushed through the gate, and both control columns were pulled back hard to bring her upon the step as quickly as possible, and so reduce the drag of water on the hull. The aircraft responded sluggishly at first, as she was laying deep in the water under her load of depth charges, anti-submarine bombs, and full fuel tanks. But as the air speed indicators flickered slowly round their dials, the uneasy motion of the aircraft steadied; and at about eighty knots, the control columns were eased forward. She then came willingly up on the step with the speed rapidly increasing, until at about one hundred knots the control columns were eased back and she came unstuck.

So, after all the long months of intensive training, we were airborne at last on our first solo operational sortie. It was to be the first of many hundreds, flown in all weathers, and all over the world.

We climbed steadily up through the crisp, clear, morning air, to clear the snow covered peaks of the North West Highlands, with the flying-boat now jerking uneasily as she felt the effects of the turbulence rising from the mountains. For a short while, there was time to settle back and enjoy the rugged beauty of the landscape passing slowly below us. But we were soon letting down to cross the Western Isles at low level; and as we coasted out across the slowly heaving grey waters of the North Atlantic, the depth charges and bombs were armed up by having their arming pins removed, and the gunners warmed up their guns by blasting a few rounds off into the sea.

A few diversions were made away from track on the way to the task area, in order to investigate the odd radar contact. It usually turned out to be a solitary drifter or trawler rolling and dipping their bows in the long green swells, always accompanied by their usual bevy of screaming wheeling gulls.

Each contact had to be thoroughly investigated, as it was well known that the Germans used quite innocent-looking trawlers to both supply their submarines with fresh supplies, and to gather intelligence of allied convoy movements, which could then be passed on to the waiting submarine packs. The spy trawlers occasionally gave themselves away by the absence of gulls, which could indicate that they had not actually been fishing, and the number or type of aerials that they carried; although these were generally concealed as far as possible behind masts or funnels if they were intelligence gathering. It was a particularly hazardous occupation for the German crews, because they were completely at the mercy of the flying-boat if detected, and one had to admire their courage.

About two hundred miles from the Scottish coast, a strong radar contact was picked up, which turned out to be Rockall as we approached it. The lonely mountain peak was bleakly jutting out of the Atlantic, with the wild sea endlessly raging up its grey sides and falling back to leave it constantly encircled by a great mass of white, heaving foam.

The position of the rock gave the navigator a convenient and accurate fix from which to start his plot. From now on it would have to rely on dead reckoning, and the occasional sunsight, if the sun was obliging enough to show its face when required.

Shortly after leaving Rockall, the engines were throttled back to cruising power in order to give us our range speed, and to conserve fuel. We then settled down to flying an in-line patrol, which it was estimated was about fifty miles in front of the mean line of advance of the convoy; and to the boring, but vitally necessary, task of searching the sea for any trace of the deadly U-boats that were devastating our shipping at that time.

After some hours of fruitless searching, we had just turned to fly a parallel track when the Tail Gunner reported that as we had banked round his turret had been covered with thick, black oil. A quick check of the engine nacelles from the astra dome showed that engine oil was pouring across the top of the wings from one of the inboard engines. There was nothing for it but to abandon the patrol and return to base as quickly as possible, because it was not possible to feather the propellers on the early Mks. of Sunderland, which meant that even with the engine switched off it would continue to windmill; and if the engine ran dry of oil, and seized up, there was every possibility that the propeller would fly off and decapitate one of the pilots. Or, even worse, the Flight Engineer.

Our first operational flight had ended prematurely, but we had gained a lot of experience and confidence, and may well have kept a threatening U-boat at bay. So, the time had not been wasted. The engine kept turning and producing some power until we had crossed the mountains of the North West Highlands and landed safely back at Invergordan.

The flying part of the course was completed with some difficulty due to the frequent interruptions caused by the unreliability of the Pegasus XVIII engines, which forced us to return to base on a number of occasions. However, it was eventually completed successfully, and we finally left Invergordan for Oban, where we were to pick up a new aircraft to fly out to join a squadron in Ceylon.

Chapter Four

Operational Training Over the North Atlantic

The heat of summer had passed and autumn was already cloaking the woods and hills above Oban with a russet-golden haze when we arrived; and there, moored on the trots which were situated between Kerrera Island and the Scottish mainland, was the now familiar sight of the Sunderlands. One of these we were to fly out to the Far East, or so I thought. But I could not have been more wrong.

Our first flight was to familiarise ourselves with the aircraft, and to carry out an air test to check its serviceability for the operational sorties that we would now be carrying out against German 'Boats' in the Atlantic before we left to join our squadron in Ceylon. However, the excitement that I experienced when climbing aboard my own aircraft for the first time, and starting the pre-flight checks, soon turned to disappointment. The bilges, which should have been reasonably dry, were all partly full of oily sea water, and had to be pumped out with the less than efficient auxiliary power unit; and then, when we finally got the aircraft airborne, we discovered that it required a lot of aileron and rudder trim in order to keep it flying straight and level. It was obvious that an aircraft in this condition would not be operationally efficient, particularly if we needed to carry out violent manoeuvres in order to get ourselves out of trouble. The out of trim condition would limit the amount of aileron and rudder control that could be applied. But at the time it was all that we were likely to get, so we decided to make the most of it. I found out later, that the aircraft had been badly damaged in a ground handling accident, which probably accounted for its wing-down attitude in flight, and the leaking hull.

A succession of air tests followed in a fruitless attempt to cure the wing-down problem and the leaking hull. But time was rapidly passing, and there was a good deal of pressure to get the aircraft and crew out to the squadron, in order to make it up to full fighting strength before the move into Burma came.

Fortunately for us, it was eventually decided that we were to change aircraft. But it was with some considerable trepidation that I waited on the deck of the control launch for the new arrival, wondering what I was going to have to cope with next.

Well, I need not have worried about it because she was brand new, delivered straight from the Shorts factory at Rochester. Her massive but graceful hull showed a gleaming white in the sunlight as she banked round over us; and the disfiguring black line that formed around the waterline of all flying-boats, and the black exhaust streaks across the top of the wings had not yet had time to form. Her four Pegasus XVIIIs sounded crisp and powerful as the sound reverberated across the water through the sharp frosty air. And painted on her pristine flanks was a large 'Z' for 'Zebra'.

We took her up for a quick air test to check her out. She handled beautifully, flying straight and level hands off, and stalling cleanly straight ahead when we pulled off the power. She would also turn on the proverbial sixpence when cranked round really hard, which was likely to come in very handy to us if we did run into trouble later on.

Altogether, I felt a great deal more confident in my aircraft when we armed up and refuelled her for our next sortie, which was to be the distant support of an Atlantic convoy even then making its slow, laborious way through the autumnal gales to Liverpool.

A chilling gale force north-easterly wind channelled furiously through the narrows between Kerrera island and the mainland, whipping the sea outside into a wilderness of foaming, white water as our power-dinghy pulled in under the stern of the aircraft. High above us, like the cabin on the stern of an ancient galleon, was the rear gun turret with its four black Brownings pointing ominously, as though in readiness towards the sky. I jumped from the swaying dinghy into the bow door, closely followed by the rest of the crew, and clanked nosily up the aluminium ladder to the flight deck.

Rain and sleet carried by a blast of freezing air stung my face as I opened up the top hatch to carry out the pre-flight check on the wings. The pre-flight also involved lowering maintenance hatches, which were situated on each side of the engines. Inside the hatches were levers that, when they were operated, opened up small fuel cocks under each tank. This allowed any water that might have formed inside the tanks, due to condensation, to run out.

I hesitated for a moment before sliding off the top of the fuselage on to the heaving, slippery wing; but it had to be done, and thankfully, as it turned out later, I drained off a good supply of fuel from each tank. Not that it made any difference to the final outcome, but at least I subsequently had the comfort of knowing that the job had been properly carried out, and that what was to happen next was not my fault.

The flying-boat's uneasy movements on her moorings, under the influence of the swirling water, began to steady as each engine coughed into life; and we began the long taxi out towards the narrows that would point us out to sea and into wind ready for take-off. As yet we were still under the lee of Kerrera island, and not feeling the effect of the wind; but as the aircraft approached the open sea, she began to feel the full force of the gale, and her motion steadily became more violent, with the bows now crashing heavily into each oncoming wave, sending out great sheets of water on each side flooding into the inboard propellers, making them shudder and vibrate, as the blade-tips sliced through the masses of green water.

Our control launch, which was attempting to follow us out, was careering wildly from side to side, and was often completely lost from view as she disappeared into deep valleys of green water.

It became increasingly obvious that any attempt to take off with this sea running would only result in disaster. So, despite the pressure to get out on task and afford some protection to the beleaguered convoy, we turned round and headed back to the relatively quiet waters of Kerrera sound, where we would have more protection from the sea. However, we would also, unfortunately, be taking off out of wind, and directly towards the hills and town of Oban. Finally, we turned on to a heading that would at least give us the best wind component, and prepared for the pre-take-off checks.

The early autumn night was already closing in, and just visible in the distance, through the flying sheets of spray and sleet, was the gloomy unlit mass of Oban, and the menacing rising hills behind it.

Although modern methods of calculating take-off distances were not available to us in those days, and I was comparatively new to flying, I already had a good idea of the distance required to get a fully laden flying-boat airborne, particularly when it was partially out of wind and faced with high, rising ground. I had no hesitation therefore, in saying no when I was asked whether I thought that there was sufficient take-off run. So the decision was made by the captain to abort the sortie. It was by far the best decision that we ever made in all our lives.

By now the wind had begun to ease down, and the flumes of white spray blown from the wave-tops were disappearing. So, once again, closely followed by a forlorn-looking control launch, we headed out to sea and into wind; and then, with no more hesitation, the four throttles were opened wide, and we began our take-off run. The aircraft which was laying low in the water under her load of heavy fuel and armament, responded slowly at first, shuddering and hesitating as each big wave smashed into her bows. But under the influence of the gale force wind, she quickly came up on the step, and with a slight pull back on the stick we were airborne at long last, and starting a slow climb up to our operating altitude.

The violent motion that we had experienced on the water had now changed to the sharp shocks of a strong gusting wind, with wet soft snow and sleet splattering against, and covering, the windscreen. It quickly rendered the windscreen wipers useless.

Thick layers of ice were rapidly building up on the top surface of the wings as I checked the operation of the de-icer boots, and then glanced back at the engine instruments glowing a dull red in the blackness of the cockpit.

It was at that moment that I felt a sudden sense of panic, and my mind momentarily went blank, as I saw that the cylinder head temperatures of the two starboard engines were dropping back fast, and that the air speed indicator was already reading less than one hundred knots.

I quickly glanced round at the two Pilots. The reason for their silence immediately became apparent. They both had the control columns hard back and were using all their strength to maintain full left rudder. I pushed both port engine throttles through the gate to give them as much power as possible, and then checked around the cockpit. Fuel cocks were correctly selected, master cocks on, magneto switches on, pitch levers were still fully fine. As far as I could see, everything was in order: it just didn't make any sense to me. But it was too late anyway, because the tail of the aircraft was already beginning to shudder and shake as it felt the turbulence burbling off the stalling wings, and the combined strength of the two pilots was insufficient to prevent the violent shaking of the control columns.

It was almost impossible to see the surface of the sea in the dense blackness of the night, and through the partially obscured windscreen. But by the greatest good luck, and the consummate skill of the captain, we stalled heavily into the water at about the right attitude, and still doing in the region of eighty knots. We landed with a crash that nearly shook my teeth out, and as we slowed to a stop the two port engines subsided into silence, leaving us helplessly wallowing in the long swell left by the passing storm, and with the aircraft already beginning to list to starboard.

It forcibly came to me as I shot down the ladder to the bomb bay to check the bilges, that if the flying-boat sank, the hydrostatically fused depth charges hanging in the bomb bay, already primed to explode when the water covered them, would make an awful big bang unless we did something about it pretty quickly.

The aldis lamp beam piercing the blackness of the night quickly revealed the reason for the list to starboard. All the tensioning wires that had supported the starboard float had snapped, and the float was bent right up away from the surface of the water. We were now in imminent danger of capsizing. I quickly plugged back into the intercom and requested that all the available crew climb out on to the port wing in order to stabilise the aircraft. It was a highly dangerous thing for them to have to do, with the wing wet and slippery from the still falling sleet and snow, and in the heavy swell that was still running. But there was no alternative if we wanted to save the aircraft and our lives; and to do them all credit, they carried it out without the slightest hesitation.

A quick check of the bilges revealed a number of bent and buckled plates with sea water gushing in through their distorted joints; but three of the bilges were still reasonably dry, which hopefully would give us sufficient buoyancy to get the flying-boat beached.

By the time that I had got the auxiliary engine fitfully pumping out the flooding bilges, and supplying us with electrical power for the lights and intercom, our control launch, which had manfully followed us out to the open sea, had already got a line on us and was taking up the tow.

I plugged back into the intercom system in order to give the captain a damage report, and was just in time to hear the exchange between the captain and the crew of the flying-boat floating dock that was luckily stationed at Kerrera island at that time. The captain requested that the floating dock be immediately flooded, in order to enable us to be towed straight in. The extraordinary reply came that the captain was at dinner and could not be disturbed. Although, as I have indicated before, our captain was a quiet and very courteous man, his language that black autumn night was an education to us all; and, needless to say, the floating dock was ready for our entrance, and the ground-crew had prepared the massive beaching legs before we were towed slowly in, fortunately before the water level had reached the depth charges.

I came to the conclusion at that point, as I watched in the dim moonlight the black oily water surging sullenly around the half submerged and battered hull, that, compared with the Sunderland Mk.III, we had but little to fear from the whole might of the Japanese Imperial Army.

There was a good deal of speculation among the crew about the cause of the mysterious engine failures, with all sorts of wild theories being put forward. But I was certain that the fuel system was the cause of the trouble because it was the only system common to all four engines.

A quick check of the fuel filters, however, once the water had been pumped out of the dock, quickly cleared up the mystery. They were full of a thick jelly which had been caused by sea water mixing with the aviation fuel; and when the fuel tanks were checked for contamination, it was discovered that they contained over two hundred gallons of sea water. So, thankfully, I was fully vindicated, having carefully drained off during the pre-flight check what would normally have been sufficient fuel from the bottom of the tanks to get rid of any water that they might have contained. Although the amount was, of course, quite inadequate to disperse such a large quantity of water.

How the sea water got into the tanks remains a mystery, as the refuelling scow used to refuel the aircraft was immediately impounded, and was found to be free of water; and a Catalina flying-boat that was recalled from on task, which had been refuelled from the same refueller, was also clear of water. The only possible logical explanation was that the aircraft had been sabotaged. This theory was dismissed by the board of enquiry, because the flying-boat trots were regularly swept by a searchlight throughout the hours of darkness; and it was assumed, from this, that a saboteur could not have been missed when climbing up on the wings. But I had been taken out fishing in Kerrera sound on several dark nights, by crafty local Scottish fishermen who knew more than a thing or two about evading the odd searchlight, and we were never detected. So it would certainly have been quite possible for a knowledgeable saboteur to climb up on a wing and quickly pump into the tanks a couple of hundred gallons of sea water without being detected.

Although it was not part of the standard pre-flight check, I decided, from then on, to always make a check for water in the fuel, especially after a refuelling had been carried out; and there were a number of occasions later on, during refuelling from doubtful sources in the Far East, when that decision stood me in very good stead.

My last thought before I dropped off to sleep for what was left of the night, was that if we had made the decision to take off towards Oban instead of heading out towards the open sea, we would certainly have crashed into the middle of the town. This would have severely curtailed all our futures, and with a few tons of high explosive on board, and a couple of thousand gallons of aviation fuel, we would probably have taken half the town with us. It didn't make for a peaceful night's sleep, and that's for sure.

Despite working night and day, it took the ground-staff nearly a month to clear the jelly out of the fuel system, and to repair the damaged float and hull. During which time we were able to enjoy the quiet peaceful beauty of the Scottish countryside in all its lovely autumn colouring, and with the more than generous help of some local Scots fishermen, a few more restful evenings fishing in Kerrera sound.

During this period of enforced inactivity, the whole crew was invited on board an American Liberty Ship by her captain, to meet his crew and have a convivial evening. He had very much appreciated the protective cover provided by the flying-boats to the convoy in which he had crossed the Atlantic, and wanted to show his appreciation.

For most of us, it was our first introduction to the lavishness of American hospitality, which proved rather too much for some of the crew. It made negotiating the companion way down the side of the ship, and the frightening jump into the darkness of the swaying dinghy, unusually difficult, when we could eventually be persuaded to leave. But it was a pleasant, good humoured evening, which certainly did a great deal for Anglo-American relations.

Eventually, the floating dock was slowly submerged and the sea water was allowed to flood in. 'Zebra', now looking very jaunty, and floating freely in her natural element once more, was towed out to her moorings, where we set about removing the pins that secured her massive beaching legs to the hull and the underside of the wings. It was just as I was leaning far out through the galley hatch in order to pull out the bottom pin, which was situated just below the water line, that we were caught by the swell generated by a passing trawler. 'Zebra' took it into her head to roll majestically over from one float to the other, which propelled me rapidly through the beam hatch into the water between the hull of the flying-boat and a large scow that had been moored alongside to collect the beaching legs.

Fortunately for me, the Co-pilot grabbed the shoulder-straps of my battle dress as I sank under the freezing cold water, and with the help of the tail gunner was able to haul me into the aircraft, looking and feeling like a drowned rat just before the scow and the flying-boat crunched together once again. It was a pretty close call, and it was not to be the last time that I would inadvertently finish up in the water. But it was certainly the most hazardous.

The ground-crew had done a first-class repair job, and after a thorough air test, during which we checked every inch of the fuel system and whether the crash had affected her handling characteristics, we were loaded up once again in readiness for another convoy distant support sortie in the North Atlantic. This time it took us twelve long, fruitless hours over a dark grey heaving sea without sighting a thing, apart from the occasional, obviously innocent, trawler, whose deck hands were pleased to see a Royal Air Force aircraft in their lonely isolation, and who would always speed us on our way with a friendly wave of the hand.

We did, however, have the satisfaction of knowing that if there were U-boat packs about in the path of the convoy, at least we would have made them keep their heads down, and use up their already depleted batteries. The sortie also confirmed that 'Z' for 'Zebra' was now as sound as a bell again, and fully ready for action.

Although the aircraft and crew were badly required by the squadron in Ceylon, in order to bring it up to strength before the move into Burma, the pressure to provide some cover for the inbound convoys, which were being devastated at that time by the German submarines which were now hunting in packs, making them much more deadly, meant that we continued to carry out a number of anti-submarine and convoy support sorties in the North Atlantic and the Iceland Faeroes gap. During this time, we marvelled at the quite extraordinary courage and endurance of the men who manned the Russian convoys, who faced sustained and quite often successful attacks by German submarines and aircraft, and the vicious freezing weather. Their life expectancy was measured in minutes in the event of them being forced to abandon ship and swim in the icy Arctic sea.

It was very pleasing for us all to know that we were now able to play some part in their protection, and it made the long wearing hours of flying through the bitter cold and darkness of the arctic night, and the turbulent violence of the winter storms, thoroughly worthwhile.

The flying under actual operational conditions also got the crew worked up to a high state of efficiency, which could not have been achieved in the same way by exercises. So that when the time came that we could be spared from the Battle of the Atlantic, and were free to leave Oban for the Far East, we were already a fairly experienced crew.

Although, as we were to find out nearly to our cost on a number of occasions later, we still had a great deal to learn.

After a short embarkation leave, which we were all very much looking forward to, during which I had to spend most of the time in London attempting to clear up my parents' bombed out house, I was pleased to leave the violent dangerous turmoil of London, and return to the relative safety of operational flying at Oban. We then prepared 'Zebra' for the long transit to Ceylon.

Chapter Five

The Transit to Ceylon

Our first stop on the transit was to be Gibraltar. It entailed the crossing of the bay of Biscay, a well known hot spot regularly patrolled by Junkers 88s and, closer inshore, ME 109s. So, although we carried more than sufficient firepower to see off an 88 if attacked, there was no point in looking for a fight unnecessarily. It was decided, therefore, to transit out at fifteen west, which would avoid the worst hazards of the bay; but to limit the time required for the trip, meant starting off from the west of Ireland. So, at long last, and after all the frustrations that we had encountered during our stay at Oban, we finally set off the following day for Castle Archdale, which is situated on the banks of the beautiful loch Erne in Northern Ireland. It was my first visit to Ireland, and although we only stayed there for a short time, the soft exquisite beauty of the countryside, and the wide variety of its abundant wildlife, made a deep impression on me; I determined that one day I would return there, hopefully in more pleasant circumstances. It turned out to be many years before I was eventually able to return, but I was certainly not disappointed when I did.

A long white line of foam and disturbed water, left by our take-off, showed up starkly against the darkening surface of Loch Erne, and great flocks of ducks and geese, fresh from their annual migration above the Arctic circle, circled the area after being so rudely disturbed by our take-off run. It was to be our last sight of the UK for over two years. But there was no time for regrets, as the aircraft had to be prepared for any eventuality that we might happen to meet. The gunners checked and warmed up their guns by firing short bursts into the sea, filling the boat with cordite fumes, and with the big Beam 5s making her shudder and shake from stem to stern as the heavy rounds were blasted off. The bomb gear was checked and primed ready to go, just in case we had the luck to catch a German U-boat on the surface of the water; and, perhaps most important of all, the galley Primuses were got going full blast, ready to provide us with a regular supply of hot coffee to keep heavy eyelids open, as the long night wore on.

In the event, however, the trip was uneventful, apart from a possible aircraft radar contact which had us all alert for about ten minutes. But eventually the early morning light showed the massive grey bulk of Gibraltar emerging out of the sea mist that was covering the straights, with the cloud formed by the Levanter wind from the east, streaming from its peak like an active volcano. We banked gently round, and with the aircraft now twitching from the turbulence flowing from the top of the rock, landed across Algeciras Bay where we taxied into the inner harbour and moored up on the trots. The first leg of the transit was safely over.

Several small snags had developed with the aircraft during the flight, which in themselves were not dangerous. But it was essential that we were fully operational for the next part of the journey across the Mediterranean sea to Malta, which was still taking an incessant pounding from the Luftwaffe, as were the unlucky convoys heading there; and there was also a very good chance of meeting up with a ME 109 or Foke Wulfe 190 during the transit. So we were able to spend a few very pleasant relaxing days on the rock, waiting for the spares to arrive, which would then bring the aircraft up to full operational efficiency.

The night that we had nearly written ourselves off at Oban had raised my blood pressure somewhat. But it was as nothing compared with the sightseeing trip of Gibraltar that was organised for us by the station padre. Sitting high on wooden benches lashed insecurely to the open back of an RAF lorry, we wound our way slowly round the narrow roads and hairpin bends of the Rock, expecting every moment to be tipped off into the harbour.

But I found the experience was very well worth it, because the amount of wildlife, which included rabbits, foxes and apes, in what appeared to be a completely alien environment, was astonishing; and although it was now late autumn, eagles and griffon vultures could still be seen hanging high in the sky, as they glided on the updraughts from the Rock across the straights of Gibraltar to the Atlas mountains of North Africa, where they could then obtain more lift to carry on with their marathon journey south. We were particularly fortunate to see the spectacular stoop of one of the Rock's resident peregrine falcons, which flashed past us down the great water catchment area on the east side of the Rock with a rushing noise like an express train, after an unfortunate pigeon.

The Alameda gardens, although close to the town centre, were a restful, peaceful place away from the crowded narrow streets. They attracted numerous, exhausted small migrating birds that were resting and feeding before continuing their long journey south. But perhaps the most interesting place to observe the migrating birds was at Europa point which attracted sea birds in large numbers. One young gannet in particular, giving a great deal of amusement to the whole crew, because he seemed to be quite unable to distinguish between something edible and a cigarette packet, until he had dived at high speed towards the object, only to realise too late what it was. He had to stall with a frantic beating of wings backwards into the water. He reminded me very much of 'Zebra's' spectacular performance that wild night at Oban, although, unlike us, he seemed quite prepared to repeat the performance.

The other remarkable feature that impressed us particularly, was the long gallery, hewn out of solid rock and about ten feet in from the almost vertical north face of Gibraltar, which had apertures cut into it for cannons. These were positioned to face and overlook the Spanish army during the great siege.

It is believed that when the Spanish queen raised her royal standard at San Rouqe in order to view the fight in comfort, the then governor of the Rock who spotted the standard from his viewpoint in the gallery, said to his officers, 'Gentlemen, cease fire. There is a lady present.' Which would have been much to the disappointment of the lady in question, I would imagine, who reputedly wasn't adverse to a little blood and thunder.

I did idly wonder, as I stood there looking out over the field of battle, if Hitler and his Panzers would behave with the same chivalry, if the king and queen raised their standard on the white cliffs of Dover, but decided that that was probably a little bit unlikely.

Gibraltar receded slowly into the distance with the Levanter still streaming from its peak, as we set off for Malta in the early morning. A strong easterly wind was whipping up the dull, grey sea into a welter of confused foam. Small fishing boats would disappear for minutes, until slowly emerging and throwing off the mass of sea water flooding from their decks.

Occasionally, there was a glimpse, through the low cloud of the long, grey shape of a destroyer or frigate, plunging her bows deep into the water, and then throwing it off like a terrier emerging from a pond. We usually took the greatest care to avoid His Majesty's warships whenever possible. It was not unknown for them to loose off the odd round at an incautious flying-boat if the fancy took them, and we couldn't rely on them always missing. But in these conditions, with the sea obscured by low cloud for long periods, and with the radar confused by the violent sea conditions, it was often difficult for us to take avoiding action in time, as we nearly found out to our cost when flying in similar conditions near the mouth of the river Pegu in Burma. On that occasion, a Royal navy cruiser blasted off a warning round at us, which came too close to our port wing for comfort, and nearly brought us to the point of the stall as we banked 'Zebra' hard round to avoid any further shots that the navy might decide to fire at us.

The turbulent weather conditions were scarcely better for us, as we were flying at five hundred feet through thick cloud, a height that would enable us to drop down quickly to sea level if we did get jumped by fighters. This strategy would keep them above the aircraft and within range of all our guns. But the low altitude also meant that we took the full brunt of the turbulence coming off the sea, making standing up or moving about almost impossible. It surprised me at the time that the Mediterranean weather, which I had always imagined to be quiet and gentle, could be so violent. But I was to experience similar conditions there on quite a few occasions in later years, so apparently it was not all that uncommon.

Finally Gozo and Malta came into view through the broken cloud, and we landed and taxied cautiously through to our moorings, between the jagged metal of the sunken freighters that littered the harbour which had only the masts and funnels showing of what had once been great cargo carrying vessels.

Malta at that time was being continuously attacked by the German Luftwaffe and Italian Air Force. So 'Zebra' was obviously going to become a prominent and inviting target sitting alone as she was in the middle of the harbour. We were, therefore, airborne again early the next day, well before first light, after once again taxiing gingerly between the sunken freighters, with only the light of an Aldis lamp shining from the bows to show us the way to open water.

My first sight of the desert came as we coasted in across the Egyptian coast on our way to Kasfariet, which was a Royal Air Force flying-boat staging post situated on the banks of the Great Bitter Lake, which forms part of the Suez Canal. The desert looked much as I had expected it to look, a dull monotonous brown stretching out to the horizon, arid and featureless, with just the occasional dust devil swirling up from the baking hot sand, which was already beginning to cover the tank tracks; and the odd burnt out tank and army vehicle that had been left motionless and blackened from the vicious battles that had taken place there.

But the surprise came as we neared the canal, to see in the distance the dead straight bright green line of cultivated and irrigated land, contrasting sharply with the bland, brown sand and rock of the desert, and looking totally incongruous in what appeared to be a completely hostile desert environment.

By now, 'Zebra' was due for a minor service, so we came to an amicable agreement with the ground-crew at Kasfariet. They would carry out the service if we would keep out of the way. We immediately honoured our side of the agreement by disappearing rapidly in the direction of Cairo on the back of a five ton truck that just happened to be going in that direction. But for me Cairo was disappointing, as it was overbearingly hot, dusty and crowded, and not many miles away the desert war was still going full blast. There were, therefore, few amusements, other than those that we had routinely been warned against by the station medical officer before leaving the UK. So it was a welcome relief after a couple of days to get back to the quiet and relatively cool air of the lakeside, where 'Zebra' had just finished her service and was looking very spruce and ready to go. Although, as we were soon to find out, appearances were deceptive.

Our next port of call was to be Habaniya, which was then the largest Royal Air Force overseas base. It was situated near the Euphrates River in Iraq. The river flows into a large freshwater lake which made it an ideal staging post for the early Imperial Airways flying-boats on their way to the Far East, and also an important strategic position for a Royal Air Force station.

We took off from Kasfariet across the Great Bitter Lake, cutting our way cleanly between two large freighters making their journey leisurely towards the canal who made much of the occasion with a great blaring of ships' sirens that could be distinctly heard above the full power roar of our four engines. Much pleased with ourselves, we climbed steadily up over the rising, bare rocky ground of the Sinai desert and headed for Iraq.

Some years later, when on the way to Singapore with a passenger-carrying York aircraft, and when Israel was still a fledgling state, we were intercepted by a potent looking Israeli Sabre jet fighter, which compelled us to reroute in the air and proceed via Aquaba. But for today we proceeded unhindered, and eventually we joined up with a major oil pipeline that was laying across the otherwise featureless top surface of the desert. We were then able to visually follow it almost all the way to Habaniya, leaving the normally overworked navigator free to take it easy for a change.

There was a worrying difference to the steady beat of 'Zebra's' engines as we neared Habaniya lake, and a slight fluctuation of boost pressure on number three engine was giving some cause for concern. So as Habaniya was now just visual in the distance, the Captain decided to carry out a straight-in approach, instead of the more usual check circuit. It was just as well that he did, because the fluctuation of boost pressure rapidly became more violent, and before we had landed the other three engines were exhibiting similar, although less violent, symptoms. Despite the loss of power on the approach, the Pilots managed a sort of controlled crash, and with the two worst affected engines shut down, were able to taxi slowly into the moorings, where a quick examination of the bilges showed a few loose rivets where water was oozing in, but no major structural damage.

So, once again, we were afflicted by a mysterious engine problem capable of affecting all four engines. But this time it wasn't the fuel system, as we all immediately expected after the engine failures at Oban, but the fact that a new type of plug washer had been fitted to the plugs during the minor servicing at Kasfariet. It should have been retightened after the engines had been run up on test. This omission had allowed all the plugs to work loose, although, fortunately for us, not before we had safely made it to Habaniya.

The three engines least affected were found to be satisfactory after the plugs had been retightened and an engine run up had been carried out. But the violent fluctuations of boost pressure in number three engine had blown a large hole through the supercharger casing, which meant that it had to be replaced with a new engine.

After a good deal of searching, a cobweb and dust covered Pegasus XVIII engine, which had probably been serviced years before for an Imperial Airways flying-boat and had laid in the corner of the hangar ever since, was discovered under a heap of debris. It certainly didn't look much, but it was all that we had, so we cleaned it up and manhandled it down to the jetty.

A three legged gantry which could be mounted on an engine nacelle for lifting off engines and propellers, was always carried on the aircraft when we were operating away from base. So there was no difficulty in removing the old engine and propeller, and then refitting the new one. But getting the engine out to the aircraft was a problem as there was no suitable Royal Air Force boat available which could reasonably be used to transport it. Eventually, after a good deal of cajoling, we were able to borrow a highly polished refuelling scow from the manager of the Russian Oil Company, who at that time carried out all the refuelling at Habaniya, after faithfully promising to return it to him in pristine condition.

We removed the propeller easily enough, and were slowly lowering the old engine which had nearly reached the deck of the scow, when a Royal Air Force launch approached us at high speed. I frantically waved them down, but they just waved back without understanding and swept by without stopping. The wash caught us and lifted the scow's bows, just as I turned round in time to see the engine emerging from a neat hole in the scow's decking.

Today, it is generally considered that the Cold War started in the 1950s, but I know better. It started that afternoon when I returned Ivan's pet scow with a gaping hole punched through her pristine decking, and it took the best part of a bottle of vodka, to restore his good humour in the mess later on that evening.

As I had anticipated, after its long sojourn in the corner of a dust covered hangar, the new engine started hesitantly, but it eventually settled down smoothly once it was thoroughly warmed up. So, after a quick taxi test in which we took the four engines up to a satisfactory full power check, we were ready for the final stage of the transit across the Persian Gulf to Korrangi Creek just outside of Karachi, in what was then India, and then down the west coast of India, across the Gulf of Cutch to Koggala, which was situated on the southern tip of Ceylon.

Now that the danger of attack by fighters was, for the time being, over, we were able to climb to a reasonable altitude where the air was cooler and fresher, and where there was less turbulence from the heating of the desert by the early morning sun. But just as we were crossing the extensive marshes in the south of Iraq, the wind which was right on the nose increased rapidly to over an astonishing one hundred miles an hour, and the desert below us was quickly obscured by a blinding sandstorm. It quickly became obvious that we would have insufficient fuel to reach Karachi if we had to battle against this wind all the way. So we made arrangements to divert to Sharjah, on the shores of the Persian Gulf, which before the war had been an Imperial Airways staging post. Hopefully, there would still be facilities for refuelling flying-boats. Eventually, however, we were forced to climb to a greater altitude in order to avoid the rising sand. We then found to our surprise that the wind speed dropped off quite quickly with only a slight gain in altitude, so we were able to continue on our planned route to India. But it was a valuable lesson for an inexperienced crew to learn: very high wind speeds can be limited to only a very narrow band of height, and can be very easily avoided if required. Today, modern jets regularly make good use of this phenomenon to limit the length of their journeys, and to save valuable fuel. But the knowledge was new to us at the time, and it certainly stood me in good stead on many occasions in later years.

The deep dark serrations of the mountains of Oman were highlighted by the brilliance of the early morning sun as we left the Persian Gulf behind and crossed the peninsular towards the Indian Ocean. It was a dramatic and quite beautiful end to our transit across the Middle East. But from now on, apart from skirting the desert of the Indian

Sind as we flew down the west coast of India, all our flying for the next two years would be carried out over either the sea or the jungle.

Chapter Six

Joining an Operational Squadron

A spattering of light rain from the low lying cumulous which was rising from the jungle in the heat of the late afternoon, partially obscured the aircraft's windscreen as we rounded Galle point on the southern tip of Ceylon, and headed for Koggala. But as the windscreen cleared, the lake and its two trots of moored Sunderland and Catalina flying-boats came into view.

The lake was divided from the sea by a narrow strip of land covered with thick vegetation and coconut trees. It was bounded by a pure white strip of coral beach which, in turn, was protected from the worst force of the great breakers rolling in from the Indian Ocean by a coral reef. The reef was low enough in places to allow the occasional big wave to flow slowly over it into a shallow, placid lagoon, so keeping the water in the lagoon fresh and crystal clear.

We banked over the lake on our down wind leg, passing low over the jungle that stretched out as far as the eye could see to the north, and finally landed at Koggala. The whole transit had taken us a long seven weeks. But despite all the problems that we had encountered on the journey, we had made it safely and in one piece, and were now ready for action. Well, it wasn't quite like that, as 'Zebra' by now was looking distinctly battered after all the indignities to which she had been subjected during the transit; and she now needed a thorough service, a wash and brush up, to get her ready for operational flying. And the crew also needed a short time to become acclimatised to the quite different life in the tropics.

Despite the damp, soporific heat and the wild, sudden intensity of the frequent monsoon storms, Koggala was a place of a quiet and overwhelming beauty that would be difficult to equal anywhere in the world. Even the camp buildings, which would normally look out of place and incongruous in such a lovely natural setting, fitted in well with their surroundings.

All the living quarters were constructed from the trunks of coconut trees that had been cut from the plantation that surrounded the camp site. The sides of the huts were covered, and the roofs thatched with palm fronds that had been plaited together to form a cool and waterproof covering. The thatched roofs had quickly become colonised by creepy-crawlies of every description, including the odd snake. Chit-chats, which are the little lizards common throughout the Far East, scuttled their engaging way across the walls, making themselves useful by catching flies and mosquitoes.

It was not at all uncommon in the early morning to hear the roar of apes as they swung their way through the overhead tree canopy. This was a warning to be very much on your guard, as they were not at all above dropping the odd coconut on an unsuspecting head if they got the opportunity, which obviously gave them a lot of amusement. But it was not much fun if you happened to be on the rather painful receiving end of it.

The lagoon was only a short walk from the campsite which, because of the protection afforded by the reef, was safe from the larger predators of the Indian Ocean. There was also a large depression formed in the reef which was continuously filled with fresh sea water as it flowed gently in from the ocean. It made an ideal and safe swimming pool. The depression had been formed by a wounded flying-boat jettisoning her depth charges after a difficult operational sortie over the Indian Ocean.

Koggala was altogether an idyllic, beautiful place, and a very far cry from the frightening, dangerous tensions of the war in Europe.

There was now a respite from flying for a short time whilst 'Zebra' was being serviced and spruced up, which gave an opportunity to explore the surrounding area. The nearest town was Galle, a famous name for centuries to mariners, for whom Galle Point was their first sight of land after probably many months at sea. Galle is also the centre of the jewellery trade, for which Sri Lanka, as it is now called, is quite rightly famous.

The Sinhalese people were gentle, courteous, and friendly, with an impressive natural dignity that was enhanced by a simple and yet very attractive national dress worn by nearly everyone. The men wore a white jacket and a form of long, white skirt, and the women a white short-sleeved bodice and a long skirt with a bare midriff.

Free from the sad conflict that now troubles the two major communities in Sri Lanka, the Sinhalese people appeared to get on well in those days with their Tamil neighbours, and indeed with us foreign intruders; although we did consider it advisable to avoid travelling about during major festivals, as the local drink, arrack, which is distilled from the coconut palm, was particularly raw and potent stuff, and could lead to the young men getting pretty excitable.

During this period of enforced idleness, when the days were beginning to drag a little, an offer was made by the head of a local community to allow one of his fishermen to take an airman out for a day's fishing in a catamaran. It was an offer that I accepted with alacrity, as a gentle day's fishing out in the quiet waters of the lagoon was just what I needed. But little did I know then what they had in mind.

The approach to the village was dominated by an enormous banyan tree, which in the half-light of the early dawn looked as though it was covered in masses of large black fruits. On closer examination, however, the fruits proved to be bats hanging upside down from the branches after spending the night out foraging. It was the only tree for miles around that was used by bats as a roost. Because of this, and its enormous size, the great tree had a deep religious significance for the Sinhalese people, as virtually everything else did in Ceylon. So it had to be treated with the greatest deference.

The small fishing village was composed of a number of attractive thatched huts, similar to those in which we were accommodated on camp. They were scattered randomly among the coconut trees which lined a beach of pure white coral sand, and in the still fresh morning air was the sharp smell of wood smoke from the village cooking fires. Drawn up on the beach were a number of fishing catamarans and their associated fishing gear, one of the catamarans still being under construction.

The hull was formed out of the trunk of the ubiquitous coconut tree, which had been flattened on one side down its length with an adze, and then turned over until the rounded side was uppermost. The trunk had then been covered with wet sacking and kept wet until the moisture had penetrated evenly into the wood, but still leaving about five centimetres of dry wood in the centre. The trunk was then again inverted and a fire kindled on the flat surface. The fire was kept continuously burning until it had penetrated in as far as the wet wood where it was unable to continue burning, thus accurately hollowing out the inside of the hull, without the weak spots that would have inevitably occurred if it had been hollowed out with an adze by eye. It was a simple, but highly effective, solution to a difficult problem. The outrigger, stays and the mast, were, of course, from the coconut tree, and the whole contraption was lashed together with coconut string and rope.

I must say that I eyed this flimsy device with some trepidation, but reasoned that as we were only going out fishing in a fairly placid lagoon, the worst that could happen to us, if it all disintegrated, was that we would have to swim ashore. But little did I know then what was in store for me.

The village head man introduced me to the crew with some formality, befitting the importance of the occasion, but we were all soon on friendly terms. The crew consisted of the Captain who only had one leg, which did nothing for my confidence. It was partially restored, however, by his quite extraordinary ability to squirt a mouthful of betal nut juice, with the greatest accuracy, over long distances, always with unerring ease; and his First Mate spent most of the time trying to emulate his superior officer, usually without success, with the result that his immediate surroundings always resembled a bloodbath.

The catamaran was quickly loaded with the necessary fishing gear, and then there was a long wait for the tide to reach its highest point. There didn't seem to me to be very much point in waiting for the tide to come in when we were only going to do a bit of fishing in the lagoon. But by now I already had an uneasy feeling in the pit of my stomach that there was more in store for me than I had originally bargained for. But it was pleasant and relaxing on the beach as we waited for the tide in the warmth and quiet of the early morning.

Eventually, however, with the help of most of the village men and a great deal of talking and laughing, most of which I fortunately couldn't understand, we were pushed into the water; and, to my surprise, the sail was hoisted. And with the catamaran quickly gathering speed, we headed straight for the reef beyond which could be heard the thunderous roar of the big breakers smashing themselves against the solid barrier of coral.

The one-legged Captain was sitting in the stern, steering and controlling the speed of the boat with such impeccable accuracy that we arrived at the reef just as a massive green breaker broke over it. When I eventually had the courage to open my eyes we were well over the reef and racing across the great swells rolling in from the Indian Ocean.

The sides of the catamaran had been raised slightly by the addition of a line of plaited coconut fronds, which gave some protection from the spray streaming off the bow wave. But I hadn't been this close to the water since 'Zebra' had subsided so elegantly on to the bottom of the dry dock at Oban. The sheer exhilaration and excitement, however, of surging down the slopes of the large waves, and of cresting the next in a flurry of white foam, soon overcame any concerns that I might have had, and to my surprise I actually began to enjoy myself.

Once we had cleared the area of confused water caused by the backwash from the reef, the motion of the catamaran became steadier and more comfortable, and we then maintained a steady course until the coast had completely disappeared from view and we were all of ten miles from land. I noted with a certain amount of returning confidence, that the rigging which was now saturated with salt water, had tightened up, and that the out-rigger and mast was swaying about a little less alarmingly, although they still looked as though they were going to fall off any minute. At this point, the sail was partially lowered and the fishing lines trolled behind the now slowly moving catamaran. The response was immediate, and quite quickly the three of us had pulled in as much fish as could be safely stored on board.

Up to then, I had been far to busy and interested in what was going on to worry about the situation that we were in. But when the fishing had finished and I had time to relax and look round, it forcibly came home to me that we were all of ten miles from land, which was completely out of sight, sitting on a hollowed-out tree trunk, with the sail and outrigger tied on with a few lengths of home-made rope, and a black threatening line of monsoon cumulous rapidly advancing towards us on the horizon.

Captain One Leg and his First Mate were quite un-moved by all this, and both calmly settled back for a lunch which consisted of cold boiled rice and fish, which had been carefully packed in little green packets of fresh banana leaves, washed down with refreshing draughts of young coconut milk. They had also, despite their obvious poverty, brought a pack for me, and jolly good it was too.

The return journey was accompanied by a fresh gusting wind and a darkening sky, and by the time that we were approaching the reef, the monsoon rain was already teeming down, dotting the long green swells with erupting fountains of glistening water, and with a dense blanket of rain completely obscuring the way ahead.

But the ominous roar of the surf breaking over the reef could be heard some miles away, and the closer we got the more turbulent and broken the water became. But I need not have worried, for with the most consummate skill, One Leg coolly positioned the catamaran so that it was poised on the leading edge of a giant breaker; and to the accompanying thunder of the tumbling, frenzied water smashing itself against the reef, we were carried over into the relatively calmer waters of the lagoon which we skimmed across at high speed, eventually sliding until we were almost high and dry on the fine white sand of the sloping beach.

In the few hours that we had been together I had built up an understanding and rapport with my two friends, and had very much come to admire and respect their outstanding courage and skill. They both reminded me of the members of my own crew, who had unhesitatingly faced a quick and unpleasant death on the slippery surface of a bouncing wing, in order to save their sinking aircraft. But it took years of travel, to many different countries of the world, before I finally came to belatedly realise that it is not the differences between people that I found to be so surprising, but their similarities.

Initially, the heat and high humidity of the south of Ceylon was exhausting for those of us who were more accustomed to the rigours of the British winter. But we soon got acclimatised, and quickly became familiar with the usual routine of banging rattan chairs hard on the floor before sitting down, in order to knock the bugs out of them, otherwise one tended to get a badly bitten bottom; or of vigorously shaking long, suede jungle boots upside down in order to remove the scorpions, or other lovelies, that had taken up residence inside them overnight.

Smoking could also be hazardous, because the tins of sealed issue cigarettes had somehow become full of weevils, which had bored a series of little holes along the length of each cigarette. The only way in which they could be effectively smoked was rather like playing a flute, with all eight fingers being used to cover up the holes. When the flame burnt down as far as one of the Weevils, however, it would explode like a firecracker, showering the onlooker with hot ash. We soon learned to keep well clear of anybody smoking.

Our breakfast toast would also occasionally behave in this unpredictable manner due to the presence of suicidal weevils, which could be thoroughly disconcerting in the early morning. However, it was, at least, a rich source of crunchy protein. But despite all these little problems, the days of inaction passed pleasantly enough, and soon 'Zebra's' servicing was complete, and she was ready once more for operational flying.

A quick air test with no armaments on board, and minimum fuel load, flown at low level round the lovely coastline of Ceylon, showed that the aircraft was fully serviceable. But the short take-off run required for a lightly laden flying-boat did not prepare us for the fact that three-quarters of the way down the flare path at Koggala was a tiny island. Although undoubtedly pretty, it was also very solid and would have to be flown around during our full load take-off, if we were to continue to be any further use to the war effort.

The following day 'Zebra' was loaded up ready for our first operational sortie in the Far East war zone. This sortie was to be an offensive anti-submarine and anti-shipping patrol, which would take us out across the Indian Ocean as far as the Andaman Islands and back; and which would also be sadly combined with a search for one of our aircraft which had failed to return from the same area on the previous day.

There was no means of knowing the fate of the crew because the Far East flying-boats operated completely on their own, and far from base. So it was never possible to determine their fate when they did not return, unless they were able to get a 'May Day' message away before ditching.

We did know, however, that a hurricane had passed through the area during the time of their patrol, which might well have been the cause of their loss. But it was much more likely that they had been intercepted by the Japanese fighters that operated out of the Andaman Islands, so it was very obvious to us that it was going to be a good idea to keep a very sharp look out, just in case any of our Japanese friends were still patrolling the area.

The early morning was windless, bright and clear, with the lagoon shining like a placid bright blue looking-glass; and three-quarters of the way down the take-off run, now looming twice as large as it had on the previous day, was the little island.

It was very obvious from the way that 'Zebra' lay low in the water under her heavy load of fuel and armaments, and with the added drag from the suction on our hull from the unruffled water, that there was not going to be sufficient room for take-off before we arrived at the island. But with one of our crews possibly still sitting in a dinghy in the middle of the Indian Ocean, relying on our efforts to save them, we had to go.

Two high speed control launches were, therefore, ordered to zig-zag across our take-off path, with the rather faint hope that their combined wakes would help to break up the smooth surface of the lagoon, and, therefore, the suction of the water on our hull, which would allow us to get the aircraft up on the step before we reached the island.

Well, it worked like a dream. We taxied as close to the edge of the lagoon as we dared, in order to give the maximum possible take-off distance, and carrying out the pre-take-off checks as we went so that we would be ready for take-off as soon as we had turned into wind. Then, as the big boat was swung round into wind under the influence of full power from the outboard engine, the other three engines were opened up to full power and we were on our way.

As soon as they heard the roar from 'Zebra's' engines, the two waiting control launches accelerated away, swaying and bouncing high into the air as they hit each other's wakes, and leaving a criss-cross pattern of foaming water across our take-off path.

'Zebra' moved sluggishly at first, only gaining speed with devastating slowness, and we had used up half the available take-off distance before we felt a severe jolt as she hit the first of the launches' wakes. It took several such jolts before she reluctantly came up on the step at about eighty knots, and then with the very limited aileron and rudder control available, the Pilots, with great skill, were able to fly her round the little island where we then had sufficient room to complete the take-off.

It was a very successful strategy and one that we were to use on a number of similar occasions after that. But the first attempt was certainly a bit nerve racking, and I did wonder at the time what the crews of the two launches thought about it, when they saw a thirty ton flying-boat, full of fuel, bombs and depth charges, rapidly approaching them at about ninety knots.

Nothing was seen of the crew of 'P', on this or any of the other sorties that we and other squadron aircraft flew in the following weeks. But the chances of visually finding a tiny life raft in the ten thousand square miles of ocean that they could have normally searched during their patrol, were virtually non-existent, as the personal locator beacon had not yet been invented. Our only search aids consisted of the Mk.I eyeball, and a rudimentary radar set which in any case would not have detected a small rubber life raft in anything less than a flat, calm sea state. So, eventually, the search had to be reluctantly abandoned.

The war against the Japanese was at long last beginning to turn in the allies' favour, with the enemy being roundly beaten at Imphal on the borders of India, and Kohima ridge in Burma. They were also being slowly but inexorably driven back across Burma. The squadron was now fully up to strength, and only waiting for a suitable base to become available before making the move into the war zone.

In the meantime, there was plenty of work on hand for the squadron to do. Convoy escorts had to be flown to protect the convoys carrying strategic supplies across the

Bay of Bengal. They were much smaller convoys than we had known in the North Atlantic, but of the greatest strategic importance none the less; and there were anti-submarine and anti-shipping patrols to be carried out over large areas of the Indian Ocean and the Bay of Bengal.

It was during this period that an operation of particular interest to the squadron crews was mounted. It involved three squadron aircraft on deployment to Redhills Lake, which is the main reservoir for Madras. Flying from there across the Chin Hills of central Burma, and landing on lakes many hundreds of miles behind the Japanese lines, there they delivered supplies and ammunition to General Wingate's men and then returned to India with his sick and wounded.

It was a particularly hazardous operation. Not only because they were operating completely on their own, without the protection of a fighter escort, a long way behind enemy lines and landing there, but because the Sunderland was essentially a low-level maritime patrol aircraft, with only a very limited ability to climb to any altitude.

In the event, only two of the squadron aircraft were able to gain sufficient height to cross the ten thousand foot high Chin Hills of central Burma, and even then, they had to thread their way between the highest of the cloud covered peaks, whilst flying on instruments.

They inevitably became known as 'Gert' and 'Daisy', after the current music-hall act of that time, and they were a first-class example of how the remarkable versatility of the flying-boat enabled an operation to be carried out deep into enemy occupied territory, which could not have been attempted by any other type of aircraft. It also said a great deal for the calibre of the men, who faced the hazards of the operation with such apparent aplomb.

The boost to the morale of General Wingate's men, who

had suffered extreme hardship in the jungle, and who had sustained severe losses from disease and enemy action, must have been incalculable when this operation was carried out by the 'Boats'. Particularly when they must have thought, at the time, that they were quite alone, and had been left to the tender mercy of the Japanese forces.

'Zebra' by now had been dropped into the Atlantic off the Scottish coast at ninety knots in a force ten gale, and had survived the controlled crash at Habaniya when the engines had given up the ghost. There was also a dirty black line round her water line that had stubbornly resisted all my attempts at removal, during one of her short visits up the slipway. So she was now looking distinctly bruised and battered.

The Pegasus XVIII engines were also suffering from problems with their valve gear, due to the high ambient temperatures in the tropics, that had resulted in us often returning from sorties with quite a few cylinders out of action.

To give the engine its due, it would still keep turning despite the loss of a few 'pots'. But the resulting loss of power, when one was possibly five hundred miles from base, and subject to possible fighter attacks where every ounce of power was needed to fight off the attack, could be a bit worrying. So, although we had all become fond of the old girl, it was with some considerable relief that we were ferried up to Korrangi creek, which is just outside of Karachi, in what was then India, to pick up a brand new Sunderland Mk.V, which we would eventually be flying into Burma.

Our new aircraft was already waiting for us when we taxied in to our moorings at Korrangi creek; and as we passed her she was slowly swinging in a circle round her moorings with the change of the tide, almost as though she was attempting to show off her graceful lines, and unblemished new white paint to the best advantage.

When I climbed aboard her for the first time, there was the potent smell of a new aircraft, and I found that she had been fitted with the much more powerful and reliable, American C4 twin Wasp engines, and markedly increased fire power by the addition of four fixed Browning .303 machine-guns in the nose.

Our old 'Zebra' had served us faithfully enough, despite the odd failing now and again. But the new aircraft with all her much more up-to-date equipment would give us a great deal more confidence in our ability to cope with whatever we would come up against in the future. Especially when we felt the immediate and powerful response there was from her four engines when we opened the throttles wide for take-off, and the crisp and certain reaction that she had to her flying controls.

We over flew the Gulf of Cutch on the way back to Koggala, carefully skirting the massive build up of cumulous nimbus cloud that often covers the area. Many years later, when I was flying over the gulf in an American Superfortress, we were incautious enough to enter a large 'cu. nimb.' at about twelve thousand feet. The devastating up currents in the cloud at that height, propelled us violently upwards to over twenty thousand feet, tearing out the wing root fillets and, with the accompanying golf ball sized hail, smashing several oil radiators. We were very lucky indeed to be able to continue on with the flight, and to make it safely to Negombo in Ceylon. So our caution on the flight back to Koggala was well justified that day.

Shortly after leaving Cutch, we were intercepted just off of Kochin, in India, by two Spitfires from the Ace of Spades squadron, which we later understood had just been withdrawn from the fighting in Burma for a short rest period.

Although we had been briefed to expect them and were keeping a sharp lookout, the first that we knew of their arrival was when one of them suddenly appeared on our starboard wing tip from out of the sun. We concluded, not unreasonably, that he was very pleased with himself for giving us all a fright, from the gestures that he made at us through his cockpit canopy. But he would have been a lot less cocky if he had realised that he was staring down the muzzles of sixteen deadly machine-guns, behind which were men who really knew how to use them, and whose trigger fingers were just itching to blast off a few rounds at an actual target for a change.

After a few minutes of reciprocal gesturing, he flicked the Spitfire over in a tight turning dive and disappeared underneath our hull, reappearing seconds later on our starboard side, and about one thousand feet above us at about four o'clock. We all knew from our training what that meant, he was going to try a standard textbook curve of pursuit attack; and, as we expected, he started the first turn in to bring his fixed forward-looking guns to bear. But curiously, instead of starting the second turn in order to allow for our forward movement, he stayed just outside the range of our guns.

Puzzled by the unusual manoeuvring, I turned to glance out of the windscreen, where all was revealed. The second Spitfire, which we had forgotten in the excitement, had taken advantage of our concentration on the first attack, and was already making a head-on charge at us. He was even then within range, and if it had been for real would have certainly by now been giving us the benefit of his eight Brownings. He did pass briefly through the sights of our Beam guns, however, and would have certainly sustained some damage from the fire of our Gunners, who had been alerted by my call over the intercom, before climbing rapidly away out of range and disappearing into some thin high cumulus.

So these lads were a whole lot smarter than we had

given them credit for, but we had an answer to their tricks. All we had to do was to drop down to sea level where, if they pressed home further attacks, they would be vulnerable to all our guns.

Well, that would have been easy, if one of them had not anticipated the manoeuvre and was already flying along underneath our hull waiting for us to descend down through his sights.

Fortunately for us, they were unaware of the extraordinary manoeuvrability of the big Sunderland and were both caught by surprise when we slammed the throttles through the gate, and cranked the aircraft round in a tight diving turn to port. This not only brought one Spitfire within range of our guns before he could accelerate away to safety, but also enabled us to drop down to wave-top height before they could recover, and where we then had them both at a disadvantage.

We spent an exciting and useful hour, carrying out fighter affiliation with them, which was useful and valuable practice for the Pilots in cranking the aircraft round in tight turns when under full power, and it also enabled the rest of the crew to become accustomed to working, and remaining orientated, under the very high G-forces that were generated in the quite often violent manoeuvres.

We also picked up a few useful tricks, which would be likely to come in very useful to us later on if we did happen to mix it with a Japanese Zero. So all in all, despite our relative inexperience against two veteran fighter pilots, we reckoned that we had come out of it just about even; and it may be, that despite their obvious self-confidence, they might even have learned a few tricks from us too.

Chapter Seven

The Squadron Moves
to Burma

The Japanese armies were eventually driven out of the Arakan province of Burma, although many pockets of determined resistance were still left behind. It had still not occurred to them at this stage that they were not invincible, and that their number was up at last. This withdrawal cleared the way for the squadron to move from Koggala to the port of Akyab in the Arakan province of southern Burma, which has a magnificent natural harbour, with plenty of sea room for flying off heavily laden flying-boats. Akyab also made a convenient starting point for our operations in the Gulf of Siam and the South China Seas, the area over which we would be operating from now on.

The transit to Akyab was made in two short hops. The first stop being made at Redhills Lake, which is situated just outside of Madras on the east coast of India. The aircraft could be refuelled there, and the lighter fuel load that was required for the shorter flights enabled all the ground-crew to be carried on the squadron aircraft, a full load of armament and as many spares as could be crammed in.

Even with her more powerful engines providing considerable extra thrust, 'Zebra' obviously felt the delaying effect of all this extra weight, because she handled sluggishly during taxiing, and accelerated away desperately slowly when under full power. But with two high-speed control launches zig-zagging across the take-off run to provide a choppy surface, and with a strong freshening wind to help her up on the step, she cleared the little island in the middle of the flare path in good style, and we were soon crossing the dense Ceylonese jungle on our way to Madras.

A blast of stifling hot air filled the aircraft when the Co-Pilot slid back his side window as we taxied up to the buoy at Redhills Lake and moored up. It should have warned me, but I opened the top escape hatch and casually put my hands on each side of the opening, in order to hoist myself up on to the top of the fuselage for a quick check on the wings and engines before I went ashore. The result was two unpleasant burns from the metal of the hot fuselage.

The wind from the north-east monsoon, whilst sweeping across central India, had collected on its way the searing heat of the Sind Desert, which coupled with the glaring midday sun had heated the metal to a burning heat. The weather was exceptional even for India, and the oppressive heat very exhausting. So we were all glad to take off again, in the comparatively cool air of the early morning for Akyab, even though we would now be entering the war zone, and subject to possible attacks from Japanese fighters and bombers.

The silt and mud washed down the rivers by the torrential monsoon rain, had painted a long, brown clear-cut stain across the blue surface of the Indian ocean. When we approached Akyab, laying at low level over the land, was a dense mass of cloud formed by the rising, hot humid air from the jungle, through which towered the menacing storm clouds of the monsoon; and contrasting sharply with the graceful beauty of the curving palms and white coral sand of the beaches of Ceylon, were the mangrove-covered mud flats, and bomb-damaged buildings surrounding the harbour. The contrast between the two coastlines was stark and ugly, making it an inauspicious introduction into what we already knew was a murderous and deadly war zone.

Already anchored in the harbour in a sheltered position was the SS *Manilla*, which was to be the support ship on which we were to live, and operate from in the coming months. She was an elderly passenger cargo boat, designed to mainly carry cargo with possibly up to twenty passengers, which meant that with all the squadron personnel, plus her own crew on board, conditions were intolerably cramped and overcrowded. The sleeping accommodation was in the hold of the vessel, where two-tier bunks were jammed close together in the airless moist heat, and the only water available for ablutions was salt sea water.

The shortage of fresh water was mainly due to all the freshwater wells in the area having been poisoned or polluted, either by the Japanese or by their friends, the Dacoits, whose favourite pastime was sneaking up on unsuspecting soldiers from behind and garrotting them.

How the wells had been approached by intruders without tracks being left in the soft mud surrounding them, was a complete puzzle to us for some time, as the mud was always only covered by the tracks of jungle animals. The mystery was eventually solved, however, by an army visitor with a wide knowledge and experience of jungle warfare who explained that the soles of Japanese jungle boots were often moulded into the shape of animal hooves. They left a realistic print in the soft ground, when worn by a knowledgeable soldier.

The result certainly fooled us, but as our visitor patiently and carefully explained, there were very few two-legged wild deer living in the Burmese jungle, which rather gave the game away to the more experienced jungle fighter. He also pointed out that the Japanese army was issued with the .22 rifle for jungle warfare. This rifle was much lighter and more manoeuvrable, but just as effective over the very short ranges in which they were used in the jungle, as the heavy and unwieldy .303 issued to allied servicemen. But it was at least comforting for us to know that they were much less effective than the .303 against low-flying aircraft, because of their shorter range.

The Heavy Conversion Unit course at Invergordan had included a certain amount of survival training, which, due to the pressure to get crews out on to the operational squadrons, had been very limited. It had also tended to concentrate on sea survival which would still be very valuable to us, of course; but as we would now be flying for many hours over enemy occupied jungle, I decided to prepare myself against the chance that we could be shot down and that I might have to survive, perhaps alone, in the jungle for many months on end.

Our very experienced army visitor was a rich source of information on edible jungle plants, and such delights as the large snails which could be found sheltering under most large leafy plants, and the mouth watering raw frog, which he claimed was particularly nutritious, and which sent him into raptures of delight at the thought of once again sampling. Caterpillars and bugs of all sorts were an excellent source of readily available protein, although brightly coloured ones had to be avoided at all costs, as they were usually highly poisonous. It was beginning to occur to me at this stage that it would probably be better to be executed by the Japanese than face that sort of cuisine perhaps for months on end, but I persevered with the questioning.

His most unusual, and perhaps most valuable piece of advice, was never to fly without at least one spare pair of clean socks, and to always wear stout leather flying boots, instead of the thin flimsy shoes that most aircrew favoured due to the continual oppressive heat. It was obviously sound advice, and as I was to find out years later, many aircrew died during the war, particularly in the desert, attempting to walk to safety through sharp desert sand. Many had to give up the attempt when their shoes were worn out and their feet became too raw to walk on. Much the same problem existed in the jungle, although this was more due to continuously wet feet rather than the sharp sand of the desert. Our issue flying footwear was the ubiquitous suede, calf-length boot, which although very valuable for warding off the malarial mosquito after dark, was much too flimsy for sustained trekking through the mud and swamp of the jungle floor. But with the judicious application of a bottle of rum to the Store's Officer at an appropriate moment, I was able to procure a good strong pair of calf-length flying boots which I was satisfied would stand up to the rigours of the jungle swamp.

The availability of water, which was probably the most important aspect of sea and desert survival, was of course not a problem in the jungle. If anything there was always a distinct surplus, especially during the monsoon. But obtaining safe, clean drinking water required some specialist knowledge. It was unlikely that it would be possible to boil water in order to make it safe, for the same reason that the frogs, snails, and other jungle delicacies had to be eaten raw, as the smoke from the inevitably damp wood would drift over a wide area and possibly give the game away to the Japanese. There were, however, a number of safe alternatives to the polluted streams, and swamp water. The emergency pack carried by all aircrew contained a very limited supply of water purifying tablets, but these would only have lasted a very short time. There was, however, the widely distributed pitcher plant that traps insects by its cup shape, where they fall into a pool of rain water at the bottom of the cup and drown. Once the insects and debris are cleaned out, the water remaining is usually safe to drink. Or there is the liana which hangs from most jungle trees; when these are cut through, there is a good flow of safe water at a convenient height to run straight into the mouth. In the areas where it would be safe to light a fire and boil water, a hollow, stout length of the widely distributed bamboo would make a suitable receptacle for both boiling water and for cooking any fish or other animal that could be trapped and caught. But it became obvious that a good knife would be essential as the issue survival knife, usually for use in a dinghy, was so shaped that it was impossible to cut the rubber of the dinghy by mistake. Unfortunately, it was almost impossible to cut anything else with it either, so it cost me another bottle of rum to obtain a suitable specimen. It also occurred to me that my .38 revolver and the ten inch knife might tend to deter any solitary Japanese soldier that I might be unfortunate to run into from being too adventurous; although my chances of actually hitting anything with the revolver were pretty remote. But he wouldn't know that.

Although it was strictly against the rules, due to the possibility of running up against the odd band of retreating Japanese soldiers or Dacoits, our Army visitor and myself were able to persuade a dinghy driver to drop us off at a suitable patch of beach. We trekked a short way into the jungle and he was able to give me a practical demonstration of the points that he had made to us at the base. It was a particularly valuable experience because it brought home to me the importance of being mentally, as well as physically, prepared for survival in the jungle. Every slight sound could be a lurking enemy, and the fear that quite innocent sounds generated could undermine one's will to survive. He was also able to point out the great difference between primary jungle, which was fairly free of undergrowth due to the absence of light filtering through the high canopy, and secondary jungle which at one time had been cleared for the growing of crops and was now overgrown and virtually impenetrable. The only way to negotiate the secondary jungle was to follow the numerous game tracks, which were easy to see. This, however, had its own dangers because the Japanese were well aware of the ease with which the paths could be used, and often prepared some accommodation for the unsuspecting escaper in the form of a concealed pit with pointed bamboo canes pointing upwards. Fortunately, these delights were restricted to areas close to the front, which I had every intention of avoiding if it was at all possible. It was also not unknown for a Japanese soldier to sit in a concealed pit on one of the few negotiable muddy tracks suitable for tanks with a five hundred pound bomb and a hammer, which he would use to detonate the bomb when a tank crossed over. It was a pretty terminal sort of activity when you come to think about it.

One of the more imaginative pleasures that the Japanese dreamt up for those aircrew who attempted to escape, other than the more usual beheading, was to pinion the unfortunate man face downwards above a patch of young, growing bamboo shoots which grow at a ferocious pace in the high temperatures and humidity of the jungle. They will penetrate anything that happens to get in the way. This method of execution had the undoubted advantage, from the Japanese point of view, that the victim took a long time to die although it is doubtful if the escaper viewed it in quite the same way.

Although the dangers and discomforts that the survivor had to face had been clearly brought home to me, the preparations that I had made, and the expert knowledge that I had acquired, gave me a certain amount of confidence in my ability to cope in the extreme conditions of the jungle. But whether I would ultimately have had the courage to survive alone in the jungle, perhaps for months on end, was fortunately never put to the test.

The sleeping accommodation on the *Manilla* was less

than perfect. However, one of the original passenger saloons had been pressed into service as a mess and dining room, which was quite pleasant. The airmen's food, though, was cooked in two field kitchens situated right up in the bows of the ship. The unfortunate airmen would have to then collect their meals, quite often in teeming rain and the teeth of a monsoon storm.

As an additional hazard, it was not at all uncommon for the food to be purloined by the odd kite hawk which would lay in wait in the ship's rigging watching the kitchens with its sharp beady eyes, and then stoop at high speed across the deck as soon as it saw the slightest opportunity, grabbing the food neatly from the helpless airman's plate and then rapidly disappearing in the distance closely followed by a string of wild profanities and a shaking of fists. The astonishing speed and sheer accuracy of those remarkable birds at low level was a source of wonder to me at the time. But I was even more surprised and impressed in later years, to see Kite Hawks, between twelve and fifteen thousand feet over India, hanging almost motionless on updraughts from the burning hot sands of the Sind Desert. From this vantage point they could presumably see their prey all those thousands of feet below, and were also able to withstand the intense cold and thin air of high altitude as well as the intensity of the heat of the Indian Sind at low level.

Entertainment on board the *Manilla* was limited to only one film, which was shown every night immediately following dinner. Its novelty tended to wear off after the first dozen viewings or so, but the appearance of the only women in the film, which lasted for all of ten seconds, was always attended by most of the squadron personnel. They would all troop out on deck in order to see her. She was always greeted with an enthusiastic waving of glasses and a loud roar of approval that reverberated deafeningly across the jungle canopy, and must have struck terror into many a retreating Japanese heart. I felt at the time that that young lady probably contributed more to the downfall of the Japanese Imperial Army than the rest of us put together.

One visit to the squadron was made by a group of ENSA entertainers, which ended prematurely when the lead player, who bore a distinct resemblance to Mr Jingle, the strolling player in Dickens's *Pickwick Papers*, pulled aside the sheet which served as a curtain to the makeshift stage, only to reveal the portly and recumbent figure of the Engineer Leader who had been draped comfortably but inelegantly across the couch which was to form the centrepiece of the show. We all quite innocently thought at first that this was part of the entertainment, and applauded with great enthusiasm. But the empty gin bottle gently rolling from one side of the deck to the other with the motion of the ship, which had just fallen from a limp and nerveless hand, led the more suspicious to conclude that there might be an alternative explanation.

Mr Jingle was not amused, and in true theatrical fashion, with his hand on his heart, declared to everybody's astonishment that he would not have his artistry abused in this way, and promptly left the ship with the rest of his company. They were accompanied down the companion way by a good deal of verbal abuse from the squadron personnel who lined the side of the ship to speed them ignominiously on their way.

The slight lapse on the part of the Engineer Leader was explained away as fatigue due to the stress of operational flying. But this ingenious theory was rather undermined by the blurred and indistinct snatches of those two fine and well known Royal Air Force ballads 'Eskimo Nell' and 'Mrs Arris' that emanated from him as he was assisted sedately away by two burly airmen.

This incident must have been the only time in which ENSA entertainers failed to live up to the reputation that they had quite rightly acquired for facing difficulties and danger with courage in order to bring some light relief to battle weary men.

The confined conditions on board the *Manilla* in the oppressive humid heat, and the difficulty of washing and bathing effectively with salt water, inevitably led to an outbreak of the usual fungal conditions that are experienced in the tropics, such as ringworm, prickly heat, foot rot, jungle sores etc. And yet, despite these small irritations, and the ever present danger of attack by Japanese bombers, and the risks generated by operational sorties carried out many hundreds of miles behind the Japanese lines, life on board settled down with good humour, and without the friction that could reasonably have been expected under such trying circumstances. This says a great deal about the calibre of the men who manned the flying-boat squadrons during the Burma war.

Apart from the other tropical delights from which I already suffered, I was also eventually laid low with jaundice. It was discovered when I reported to the sick bay for some inoculations. The Medical Officer immediately detected the jaundice from the bright yellow colour of the whites of my eyes, which I had attributed to the mepagrine drug that we had been taking as a defence against malaria. The uncomfortable indigestion that accompanies the illness I had put down to the delights served up on board the aircraft in flight.

The iron will of the Medical Officer immediately confined me to a single cabin in the sick bay and to a very limited diet of poached egg, jelly, copious quantities of Epsom Salts, and positively no alcohol.

This last penance, however, was partially overcome one evening when a curious rattling noise, which appeared to come from the cabin ventilator, turned out to be a bottle of scotch suspended on the end of a length of string. A thick and rather slurred conspiratorial whisper echoing down the shaft, which could have been quite reasonably heard from Akyab to Rangoon, wished me well. Unfortunately, it was also heard by the rest of the ship's company who had been as mystified by the muffled laughing and milling about around the ship's ventilator as I was. The Medical Officer promptly relieved me of the whiskey, of course, although not before I had fortified myself with a good proportion of the contents.

The fresh poached eggs which I ate with such distaste were unobtainable on board the *Manilla*. But I learned later that the Medical Officer had personally obtained them by scouring the villages in the local countryside at considerable personal risk to himself from marauding bands of retreating Japanese soldiers and Dacoits. Such was the level of commitment of squadron personnel to each other in those difficult days.

The jaundice proved to be very unpleasant. But I was much more upset at the thought of a Flight Engineer from another crew having to fly in my place, particularly on a hazardous operational sortie. It hurt my pride, and I felt that I had let down the crew. But the only sortie flown by the crew while I was in dock was an anti-submarine patrol off the Andaman Islands, which as it turned out was quite uneventful; and to my overwhelming relief, I eventually heard the roar of 'Zebra's' engines overhead as she returned safely to base.

Although Akyab harbour was conveniently positioned for operational sorties in the Gulf of Siam and the Indian Ocean, and was well forward of any airstrips available to the Transport Command Dakotas which were doing such sterling work by supplying the Chinese troops and the Fourteenth Army over the Burma Hump, it was far from perfect for arming up and refuelling flying-boats. The wide, southern entrance was exposed to the full force of the monsoon, which, particularly when the tide was changing, would result in a deep swell accompanied by a violent chop, making it almost impossible to bring an unwieldy bomb scow or refueller alongside an aircraft without some damage being caused. 'Zebra' was now suffering the indignity of being battered by out of control bomb and refuelling scows as they tried to come alongside in the heavy swells, which was buckling and denting her curving chines and scratching her once immaculate paintwork. But it was a great testimony to her builders, Short Bros. of Rochester, that apart from a few loose rivets which were quickly and easily tightened up, she remained watertight, and when airborne flew straight and level hands off, just as she had done when we had first flown her.

There were few duties to be carried out when not flying, apart from keeping the interior of the aircraft clean, in which the whole crew was involved, including the officers, and keeping jabs and flying equipment up to date.

The Pilots and Flight Engineers were the only members of the crew with sufficient technical knowledge to be able to start the engines and keep the flying-boat from breaking her moorings in the event of one of the severe storms that afflict that part of the Indian Ocean. They were, therefore, elected to mount the nightly boat guards, which involved a solitary and lonely all-night vigil. The moorings had to be checked hourly, and any intruders that might happen by fought off with the aircrew issue .38 revolver with which we were all issued.

It forcibly struck me at the time, as I listened nervously to the rattling of the moorings and the creaking of the big hull in the blackness of the night, that this last requirement was a bit unlikely in my case. Particularly as my only claim to fame as an expert marksman came from nearly shooting the Gunnery Officer in the foot on the firing range.

Fortunately, all the boat guards passed off without major

incident, although I found it particularly upsetting one dark stormy night when making an hourly check of the moorings. As I pushed away with the boat hook, what appeared to be a bundle of flotsam caught up around the buoy, turned out to be a corpse that had been distended in the heat, and had floated down the river from the battles that were still taking place upstream. But apart from that unpleasant incident, which didn't do much for my nervous system, my faltering courage was fortunately not put to the test.

During one of my boat guards some months later, however, when the squadron had moved from Akyab to Syriam, which was on the banks of the Pegu River and about ten miles upstream from Rangoon, I thought I heard above the noise of the river in flood, and the creaking and buffeting of the big hull as it moved restlessly on its moorings, some scratching and bumping noises. They sounded for all the world like the banging of a dingy or, worse still, a Dacoit canoe against the side of the metal hull.

With all my old fears aroused, I summoned up what was left of my flagging courage, and crept as quietly as I could up the aluminium ladder to the flight deck, where I peered fearfully and uncertainly out through the windscreen at the black, rushing water. The night was very dark, with only the odd glimpse of a fitful moon through gaps in the racing cloud cover; and the tree-lined banks of the river were shrouded in a deep, menacing darkness. So there was little to be seen; and with the Japanese now in full retreat, and attempting to escape across the river after dark, it would have been far too dangerous to use the Aldis lamp to light up the area.

As I stood there, wondering what on earth to do next, there was a distinct and loud bang from the general direction of the galley. So, drawing my revolver and pointing it in what I hoped was roughly the right direction, I crept quietly down the ladder to the bottom deck, and edged my way slowly through the wardroom – rather after the style of James Cagney, I thought, although he always seemed to manage to keep his revolver from shaking.

I hesitated on the threshold to the galley for a short while, whilst straining my ears to detect the slightest sound above the noise of the river. But it all seemed quiet enough. So, taking my courage in both hands, I shone the torch around; and there, laying on the floor of the galley, was the tin of condensed milk that I had recently opened to make myself a cup of tea, and disappearing rapidly up a pipe in the direction of the wing root was a big grey water rat. He paused for a second or two, turned and looked at me intently with large unblinking brown eyes, and then in an almost leisurely way turned and carried on up the pipe. I must say that he appeared to be a jolly sight more composed than I was.

Although the little devil had just given me the fright of my life, I couldn't help admiring the cool courage that he had shown in facing up to me in what must have been just as frightening a situation for him. But, as we were to find out later, he was made of pretty stern stuff; and when he finally decided to leave the aircraft some months later I was surprisingly sorry to see him go.

But at least the strange mystery of the bumps in the night was solved. We now had a new crew member on board. Little did I realise at the time, though, what a problem he would turn out to be in the future. Anyhow, for the time being we had more than enough to worry about, until Ratty eventually decided to join the crew at Syriam.

Top: 'T' high and dry, on the mudflats.
Bottom: The author with 'Zebra' in the background.

Top: Rangoon's POW camp.
Bottom: Rangoon's Buddhist temple.

Top: Mk. Vs.on the trots at Koggala.
Bottom: The ill-fated 'P', just prior to her disappearance.
Photographs courtesy of RAF Museum, ref. no. P2004 and P2202.

Top: Sunderland Mk. IIIs.on the slipway at Short Bros' Belfast.
Note the newly flared step and the massive beaching gear.
Bottom: 'Zebra''s cockpit.
Photographs courtesy of Short Bros, Belfast.

Sunderland Mk. V.

Sunderland Mk. III.
The mid-upper and nose turrets and the triangular bomb bay hatch
underneath the starboard wing can be seen clearly.
Photograph courtesy of Short Bros, Belfast.

Chapter Eight

'Operation Dracula': The Retaking of Rangoon

The squadron now continued with the same anti-submarine and anti-shipping patrols over the Indian Ocean and the Bay of Bengal that it had carried out from its base in Ceylon. This was, however, now from a much more advantageous position, because the transit distances were much shorter. Offensive anti-shipping patrols could also be carried out, with the squadron aircraft penetrating deeply down into the Gulf of Siam, across which shipping was carrying vital war supplies to the Japanese army in Malaya from the then named Indo China.

The operations flown by the squadron in the gulf became so regular, that they became known on the squadron as the 'milk run'. But when the Japanese realised what was going on they reacted very unsportingly, we thought, by heavily arming some of the vessels and increasing their fighter activity in the area. So it very quickly became a lot less like delivering the daily milk supply, which a few of our aircraft was to unfortunately find out. Not all of our trips were routine, however, as our next sortie was to show.

There was always a long pre-flight check to be carried out by the Flight Engineer before take-off, so it was my policy to always arrive at the aircraft well before the rest of the crew in order to give plenty of time to carry out the check thoroughly. I would then rely on the Captain and Navigator for my briefing when they arrived at the aircraft. On this occasion, however, I had been called into the makeshift Ops. Room early on in order to calculate a new fuel and bomb load for a shorter detail than we had been used to.

I looked enquiringly at the navigator as I went in, who just pointed to his chart by way of explanation. Instead of the long line across the Indian Ocean that I had expected, which would have taken us as far as the Andaman Islands, and then skirting Car Nicobar on the way back, the black line made straight for the Delta of the Pegu River, and there turned inland to make a bee line for Rangoon.

When I looked up from the chart I took an anxious longer look at the Navigator. 'It's okay,' he said confidently. 'The Fourteenth Army will be arriving there today, and the Japs are bound to have gone by then.' Well, I wasn't all that convinced and that's for sure, having learnt by then never to believe anything that I heard and only half of what I saw when it came to intelligence briefings. But it would be a change from the routine anti-submarine patrols to which we had become accustomed, and it was my guess that this affair was likely to be a pretty lively one.

My suspicion of intelligence briefings stemmed from the secrecy that surrounded any wartime operation in which crews were briefed on a need to know basis. This usually meant, in practice, that on occasion important information was omitted at briefings by over-cautious intelligence officers.

For example, some time after the Far East war had ended, the crew belatedly discovered, quite by accident, that a British submarine had cached weapons and supplies of food and water on several of the deserted islands in the Gulf of Siam. This was to enable shot-down aircrew who were able to make it to one of the islands in their dinghy to survive and hopefully evade capture. This knowledge may well have enabled some of our crews to have survived until the war had ended, if they had only known about it.

The objective of 'Operation Dracula', in which we were to take part, was to reinforce the Fourteenth Army, then fighting its way against the most stubborn resistance through the jungle, from the West with a large Naval task force entering Rangoon from the South.

Our task was to survey the deep water channels in the Pegu Delta, which through years of wartime neglect had become silted up, and then mark the deeper channels, which could be easily identified from the air by the deeper blue colour of the water.

As I climbed out of the swaying dinghy into the bow door of 'Zebra', a low steamy mist was drifting off the jungle, covering the harbour and partially concealing the long grey shapes of the warships which were anchored further out in the deeper water towards the entrance. The mist would make take-off tricky, not only because of the difficulty of seeing the anchored ships, but also because of the large amount of debris that was continuously being washed down in the rivers that entered the harbour because of the monsoon rains. The debris occasionally included very large tree trunks, which would be difficult to spot in the reduced visibility, and could easily rip the bottom out of a flying-boat if she hit one at eighty or ninety knots. But dawn comes quickly in the tropics, so hopefully the rising sun would quickly burn off the steamy mist; and already the early morning light was beginning to glow luminously across the still water.

The rest of the crew were still at their briefing. So, 'Zebra' was laying quietly on the water as I carried out my pre-flight checks, apart from the rattling of the moorings and the creaking of the huge hull as it occasionally rolled over from one float to the other by the action of the swell.

She was already fuelled and armed up, ready for action; and the long lines of .303 ammunition were waiting ready in their racks, to be loaded into the guns at the last moment by the Gunners.

Hanging in the bomb bay just above my head as I passed through, were the eight deadly 250lb. depth charges and anti-submarine bombs that we had every intention of depositing on any Japanese ship or submarine that happened to get in our way during the sortie.

The quiet was eventually broken by the high pitched revving of a power dinghy engine, as the driver reversed it to bring the dinghy neatly to a stop alongside the bow door; and then came the loud clanging of jungle boots on the metal flooring as the rest of the crew poured aboard to take up their various crew positions.

The Gunners climbed into their turrets and completed the arming up of their guns and the final polishing of the turret perspex. Even the slightest spot or scratch on the perspex might be mistaken for an enemy fighter, particularly when a Gunner was tired, or had been disorientated by high Gs.

The high G was always much worse for the tail-end Charlie, stuck right out on the end of the tail as he was. Its effect could often result in a mistaken blast of fire by the Gunner, as he identified a speck on his turret perspex as an attacking fighter. The sudden unexpected blast of noise from the guns would send a cloud of cordite fumes through the aircraft, shake the tail from the violent recoil of the four Brownings, raise everybody's blood pressure, and, worst of all, cause unnecessary expenditure of vital ammunition, which might be needed later to fight off a genuine attack.

Up on the flight deck the Pilots were checking the operation of the flying controls, and the Navigator was laying out his charts in a hurry. From now on he would be working flat out, with only a magnetic compass and dead reckoning to navigate us at low level through the intensity of the monsoon storms and across the hilly countryside to Rangoon.

There was a sharp, incise clicking from the Wireless Operator's position as he checked in with his control, and a soft green glow showed through a gap in the partly drawn curtains round the radar set. The radar, although primitive compared to the sets that we eventually received, was still of considerable value in detecting targets which lay out of range of the Mk.I eyeball. With a skilled operator it could even be used to detect the violent turbulence in the centre of cumulous nimbus clouds, although experience had quickly taught us, with the onset of the monsoon, that the violent twitching of the airframe as we approached a large cu. meant trouble; and it was always a wise precaution to make a small diversion round the cloud in order to avoid its hard centre.

From the direction of the galley came the welcome roar of the twin Primuses warming up the first coffee of the day; and right up in the nose, one of the Gunners had retracted the twin-gun turret to allow himself room to get to the moorings.

The aircraft was normally secured to the buoy by a strong chain which was secured to an eyebolt on the keel at one end and the mooring chain at the other. This arrangement, despite being immensely strong, nevertheless took far too long to release once the engines had been started and the flying-boat was tugging at the moorings. It was also impossible to reattach the wire hawser quickly enough to the keel when the aircraft taxied up to the buoy and the engines were cut, which was a very critical moment.

To enable the aircraft to be slipped quickly and easily from its moorings, therefore, a short slip was used. This was a short but substantial length of rope which was threaded with a boathook through a large loop of cable on top of the buoy. Each looped end of the short slip was then placed over the aircraft's bollard. One loop of the short slip could then be quickly and easily slipped from the aircraft's bollard when the engines were started, and we were under our own control.

When the aircraft returned to the moorings, the short slip was then threaded back through the loop of cable on top of the buoy with a boat hook, although now with more difficulty, and the permanent moorings could then be secured at leisure.

Mooring up and slipping the moorings of a big flying-boat, especially in a gale force wind, when the bows of the boat and the buoy could be falling and rising some feet and the moorsman was partially blinded with rain or sleet, was a very skilful and dangerous job, and a great deal of experience and co-operation with the Pilot was required to carry it out competently.

It was not unknown for the Flight Engineer to be given the signal from the Captain to 'cut engines' during mooring up, only to belatedly find out as the engines fell silent that the short slip had not been properly secured and that the aircraft was already drifting back all on its own with the tide. More often than not, between two trots of closely moored up flying-boats, there would then be a wild panic on the flight deck to get the engines started up again before half the squadron aircraft got written off by the maverick aircraft.

On fast flowing rivers in the tropics, which were often swollen by the monsoon rains or with the combination of a particularly strong wind and tide, it would sometimes be impossible for the Pilot to judge exactly the right amount of power to use to loosen the short slip sufficiently to allow it to be freed, but not so much power that the bow would be forced hard up against the buoy, again making it impossible to slip. In this case, the only alternative was to cut the rope with a fire axe. This we had to do on more than one occasion.

Once the aircraft was slipped from the buoy and we were under our own power, the bollard was unbolted and lowered, which in turn allowed the front turret to be wound forward and locked in position ready for use.

A cloud of blue smoke, quickly whipped away by the breeze, swirled from 'Zebra's' port outer exhausts as the engine coughed hesitantly into life. But it settled down smoothly with all the temperatures and pressures normal as the other three engines started up. With the electrical power now being supplied by the aircraft's generators, I shut down the auxiliary power unit. The short slip was quickly released, and with an exuberant burst of power from the starboard outer, the Captain swung her head round into wind, and we started the taxi out to our take-off position. The subdued noises made by the crew's pre-flight checks were now submerged by the roar and vibration from the four twin Wasps, which reached a deafening roar of sound as we took each pair of engines up to combat power to check their performance. And then, with all pre-take-off checks and the engine run up complete, we were ready for take-off.

As I had previously suspected, the early morning mist had been cleared by the heat of the rising sun, and laying dead ahead of us was a promising gap between two long grey frigates, which was just about wide enough for us to get through with a bit of room to spare. It would have been great fun for us to reverse the roles for a change, and to have given His Majesty's Royal Navy a fright by charging at high speed through the gap. But the Sunderland looked too much like a Japanese 'Emily' flying-boat for us to take a chance on not being recognised as a British aircraft. We were already very aware that Matelot's trigger fingers were always nervously on the trigger, so we opted for a slightly out of wind take-off instead. It was probably just as well, if the muzzles of the anti-aircraft guns that so ominously followed us round as we taxied by were anything to go by.

With the open sea ahead of us, 'Zebra' now began to feel the effect of the big rollers punching in from the Indian Ocean, and the spray from her bow chines as she dipped her bows into the glassy green slopes, was swirling through the inboard props making them shudder and vibrate. So, it was now time to go.

All four engines were opened up to take-off power, to which the aircraft responded eagerly; and with the extra thrust from the large waves striking the bottom of her hull, we were soon up on the step. With a gentle ease back on the stick at about ninety to a hundred knots, she came unstuck. For good or bad, we were now on our way to Rangoon, and what it had to offer us.

The transit to the mouth of the Pegu River would take us about three hours, cruising at five hundred feet over the sea all the way. We would just be skirting Ramree Island, on which it was suspected there was a Japanese fighter airfield, so no time could be lost in setting up the aircraft ready for action.

The Navigator had already armed the bombs and depth charges before take-off by removing the arming pins, and the Gunners had loaded the long lines of .303 ammunition into the magazines of their guns. All that was now needed was to warm up the guns and check them for stoppages.

Each crew member was now cocooned in his turret or crew position by the continual roar from the noise of the four engines, which was only occasionally interrupted by the click of a microphone and a crackling of static as an intercom was switched on to pass a terse command. Silence on the intercom except when necessary messages were being passed was absolutely vital, as at any moment we might come under attack, and an immediate response by the whole crew acting together might well save the day.

One quickly learned to identify the sounds made by the different intercoms as they were switched on. The rush of noise made by the four engine slipstreams rushing past the tail Gunner's position being particularly heart stopping, because one never knew what was coming next, and it could well be the report of a fighter attack.

With the engines nicely settled down and all the aircraft systems operating normally, the Flight Engineer's panel was taken over by the Second Engineer, whilst I went forward to check the operation of the front turret and its guns. The perspex canopy was clean and polished, and the turret operated smoothly and quickly under the influence of the twist-grip control. A round pan of ammunition was already in position on top of each breech block if the pan jammed or there was a gun stoppage during firing, or when the pan ran out of ammunition. It was a simple matter, taking only a few seconds to replace the pan with another from those clipped round the sides of the turret.

The Pilot let down to fifty feet above the curling wave-tops when I requested permission to warm up the guns. This was a signal for all the Gunners to blast off a few rounds, including the four fixed Brownings situated just below my feet which were fired by the First Pilot.

'Zebra' shook violently from one end to the other, as if shaken by some giant hand, when the guns blasted their shells into the surrounding sea, leaving behind the aircraft on the surface of the water a large area of white, boiling foam, and the aircraft filled with the sharp acrid smells of cordite and hot gun oil. The noise throughout the aircraft was deafening, but it was very comforting to watch an exhibition of the massive fire power available to us if we did run into trouble during the trip.

To make adequate allowance for our forward move-ment, I positioned the red glowing ring of the gunsight just in front of a large tree trunk, that was slowly rising and dipping with the big swell, about five hundred metres in front of us.

When I squeezed the trigger the two machine guns poured out their rounds without hesitation, sending up a line of splashes in the water just beyond the tree trunk. It was a near miss, but I was quite satisfied that if it had been a submarine or a ship it would certainly have been caught in the cone of fire formed by the recoiling guns, which would have been pretty unhealthy for it with eighteen hundred rounds a minute pumping in.

With the exception of the Navigator who was working furiously over his charts, there was little now for anybody else to do until we got to the Pegu, except keep a sharp lookout for fighters. The only interruption to our steady progress came as we carried out a couple of three drift winds to enable the Navigator to assess an accurate wind component.

A three drift wind was carried out by dropping a smoke float in the sea, which was then approached from three different headings one hundred and twenty degrees apart, the drift being assessed from the drift sight each time that we flew over the top of the smoke float. It was a long and time consuming diversion from a patrol or transit which could well have been more usefully employed, and it always considerably lengthened the transit time. But it was very vital to assess the correct wind component if accurate navigation was to be carried out by the Navigator. It was normally quite common practice, if the sea was at all choppy, for the Pilot to make a sufficiently accurate assessment of the drift from the direction of the spume blown from the wave-tops. But today, a correctly timed rendezvous with the navy ships was important, as they tended to be highly suspicious of late arrivals, quite often reacting with the odd warning shot across the bows. This could be a bit unsettling when you were both supposed to be on the same side; but I can't say that I really blamed them under the circumstances, when seconds could make the difference between life and death.

A long dark coastline slowly became separated from the low lying cloud, as we approached the Delta of the Irawaddy, which we crossed without incident. The surrounding countryside appeared to be lifeless, apart from a few farmers working with their slow moving oxen in the paddy fields, up to their knees in water. They scarcely gave us a glance as we passed overhead, which suggested that they were used to seeing aircraft about. Not a particularly comforting thought for us, as the only aircraft in the area, at that stage of the war, would have been Japanese; although that was to quickly alter from now on. But we soon cleared the Delta, and about ten miles ahead lay the long grey shapes of the task force waiting for us at the mouth of the Pegu.

Radio silence was now in force to save giving the game away to the Japanese forces. Our signaller was already positioned in the astra dome transmitting what we hoped were the correct letters of the day with the Aldis lamp. To make quite sure that we were really welcome, however, we circled the force at low level a cautious five miles away until there was an answering blinking from the task commander's ship, giving us the all clear to approach and carry out our reconnaissance. We made several exploratory orbits of the Delta, which covered a very large area. It quickly became obvious from the deeper blue colour of the water, which was the most suitable channel for the task force to negotiate, so we let down to fifty feet and dropped a line of smoke floats along the channel, indicating the best route for the ships to take, until we had reached the deeper water of the main river, where the force could then proceed safely and freely.

As we turned back towards the force, a destroyer was already turning out of the line of ships with a mass of white foam churning from her stern. She was obviously going to be the lucky one to have the first go. We all held our collective breaths as she cautiously entered the channel that we had already marked out, closely followed by the rest of the force. If any of them got stuck now, they would be sitting ducks for any passing Japanese bomber, and it could all turn into a disaster. But they all passed slowly and safely through the shallow section of the delta, and then assembled in line astern when they had reached the deeper water. A thank you blinked from the control tower of the task commander's ship, then cleared us to resume our sortie.

As we banked round on leaving the task force to bring us on to a heading that would take us on to Rangoon, a bright flash of light in the distance caught my eye, which could possibly be the reflection from a fighter windscreen. It was quickly concealed by the banks of fluffy white cloud through which we were intermittently flying; but as we got closer to the city and the cloud layer began to thin out. It became obvious that it had been a reflection of the bright sun on the great golden dome of Rangoon's Buddhist temple. It was a spectacular and impressive sight from the air, and certainly a very considerable improvement on the possible alternative – a Japanese Zero.

Three low level orbits around the city revealed few signs of life, and certainly none of the frenzied activity that could have been expected from a newly liberated town. There was, however, a lot of waving and wild gesticulating from a large crowd of raggedy dressed men; who were stood outside a number of two storey buildings, which were curiously positioned like the spokes of a wheel round a central square, the whole area being surrounded by high wire fences. The third circuit, which took us directly over the buildings, revealed that painted on the roof in large white letters, were the words BRITISH HERE. So it was Rangoon's prisoner of war camp. The prisoners would have spotted the RAF's red, white and blue rondells on 'Zebra's' flanks, and would have realised that there was a British aircraft flying overhead; and that their dreadful ordeal was nearly over, which must have accounted for their wild excitement. It was a wonderful moment for the whole crew to realise. We had brought some hope to the poor men, many of whom had been imprisoned for four years or more under the most appalling and degrading conditions. But despite the euphoria of the moment, the realisation was also just beginning to dawn on us that, quite contrary to the confident briefing that we had received before leaving the SS *Manilla*, the Fourteenth Army had still not arrived in Rangoon, and that we were flying at low level around a possible enemy occupied city, casually enjoying the view.

It was becoming quite obvious to us that if the Japanese army had still been in command of the city, 'Zebra's' hull by now would have been a whole lot less watertight. A hurried conference was, therefore, held on the flight deck, chaired by the squadron Commanding Officer, who had come along to see the fun; and the decision was made to take a chance and set down on the River Pegu, right in the middle of the town.

We flew at low level along the surface of the river, dropping a series of smoke floats into the water as we went, in order to roughly assess the wind speed and direction from the smoke. There was, of course, a strong cross wind blowing across the river as we prepared to touch down, and 'Zebra' was crabbing towards the water with her bows pointing towards the river bank, rather than upstream. But with his usual outstanding skill, the captain kicked her straight just at the moment of touch down, and our keel sliced cleanly through the racing river until she slowed to a stop in the usual flurry of white foam.

A great deal of power was required to taxi the aircraft against the fast flowing current produced by the monsoon-swollen river. But eventually, after several abortive tries, we managed to get moored securely to a large shipping buoy which was situated right slap bang in the middle of Rangoon. So, after five long years of war the British were back, and we were the first to get there.

After a lot of gesticulating and shouting across the water, a local boatman was eventually persuaded that we were not actually going to cut his throat, although we must have looked remarkably like a lot of rather scruffy bandits, and he agreed to take us ashore. He was also able to assure us that the Japanese had vacated the town just that morning. So it had been a pretty close call, and one that I hoped was not likely to be repeated in the future, because I was distinctly not in favour of having my head lopped off. That was the fate quite often reserved for shot down aircrew by the Japanese, after they reputedly found that at least one crew were carrying dum-dum bullets loaded into their revolvers.

The rumour was very unlikely to be true, but if there had been any truth in it, there was some justification for the Japanese action because the dum-dum bullet was made to spread on impact, so quite deliberately causing a dreadful wound to the unfortunate victim.

Although a city that had been occupied by an uncaring and vicious enemy for some years was not likely to be tidy and well cared for it came as some surprise to us to see just how badly it had deteriorated. The strong smell of death and of the rotting grain in the damaged warehouses, and the rubbish in the streets, was all-pervading. Curiously, bags of rotting rubbish had been tied in rows, and were hanging from the ornate iron railings that lined the river bank. Once we got ashore, however, we discovered that they were not bags of rubbish, but corpses, many of whom were Japanese soldiers, as well as the local people. They had all been executed by the retreating army by having hessian bags tied round their necks and then being thrown over the railings to hang in torment until they were dead. The awful scene did not endear us to the Japanese any more, that is for sure; and when on later sorties, after bombing and machine-gunning the Japanese shipping that we discovered in the Gulf of Siam, I found it impossible to feel any pity for the dead that we left behind us, when I knew that they were capable of such appalling atrocities.

Much later, after the Japanese had surrendered, I witnessed in a number of Far Eastern countries the arrogant brutality with which the Japanese officers treated even their own men, frequently striking them full in the face for some slight or imagined misdemeanour. It is perhaps not too surprising that they, in their turn, treated their prisoners of war, and often the local population, with such savage and indiscriminate cruelty, when they had the opportunity to impose their will on them, without having to suffer the consequences of their dreadful crimes.

We made a short sightseeing visit to the temple, whose glittering dome had given me such a fright earlier on, but the smell of rotting flesh, and the general air of utter deprivation and ruin, quickly sent us back to 'Zebra' and the fresh clean air of the river.

Night falls quickly in the tropics, and the darkness thankfully shut out the tragic sight of the decomposing corpses hanging on the river banks. The tropical evening was hot and sultry, with only the occasional glimpse of a bright moon through gaps in the cloud cover. Most of the crew chose to lay out on the wings, which were cooled by a gentle breeze.

Rangoon, which was silent with not a light showing, had completely disappeared in the gloom; and although the city was only half a mile away from us across the water, it seemed as though we were completely alone and isolated on our watery world. The only occasional sign of life came from the sudden appearance out of the darkness of a ghostly fishing boat or overloaded sampan, as they drifted silently past us on the tide and quickly disappeared into the all-enveloping darkness.

Our Wireless Operator, who by some magic known only to himself, had laid an intercom headset on the wing between us and had connected it to his WT set, which, with great skill, he was able to tune into All India Radio.

Through the insistent crackling and fading of the static from the headphones came the nostalgic and indistinct sound of a dance band. It seemed incongruous and strange in that bizarre setting. Eventually, however, the music faded into silence and an announcer started to read the war news, which immediately captured all our attention. Through the fading and general background noise from the headphones, I thought I heard him say: 'Today, Germany has capitulated unconditionally to the Allies. The war in Europe is now over.'

We were all so utterly stunned by the sudden unexpected and dramatic news, that for a time nobody moved or spoke. We had been so completely isolated and preoccupied with the trauma of our own war, that not one of us had had an inkling that the end of the European war was even close.

Scarcely daring to believe what I had just heard, I turned excitedly to speak to the navigator, who was sitting close beside me on the wing. He was silhouetted against the now bright moonlight with his head sunk deeply in his hands, and his shoulders were shaking. The intense emotion that he now felt, from knowing that after all these long brutal years of war, his wife and family from whom he had been separated for so long, were safe at last, had been too much for him, and it had broken through his normally natural reserve. I quietly left him and joined the rest of the crew, leaving him alone to the comfort of his thoughts and memories.

It was the only time in the two years that I was privileged to serve with that crew that I witnessed any one of them betray the slightest sign of fear, nerves or emotion, although there were many occasions when they could have quite reasonably have done so.

It had been a very exciting, but long and tiring day, so most of the crew settled down early to get as much rest as they could on the aircraft's metal flooring. I was better off than most, as with the most unusual foresight I had bagged the canvas cockpit cover early on, into which I was able to snuggle on the floor of the flight deck.

The Commanding Officer, as befitting the great man, had taken over the canvas bunk in the wardroom; so, for the time being at least, peace descended on 'Zebra' as she lay there on the moonlit water, with the fierce current tugging hungrily at her moorings, and there was only an occasional rumbling as a floating log or mass of debris rubbed along the side of her metal flanks.

Despite the unaccustomed comfort of the canvas cockpit cover, and my tiredness from the long exciting day, I remember now that after hearing that wonderful news on the radio sleep was a long time coming to me that night on the Pegu. I could at long last allow myself the luxury of thinking thoughts that I had not dared to think before: about possible survival from the war, and the joy of eventually returning home to my family in England. And if the subdued voices of the crew in the wardroom and the endless cups of coffee that they brewed up were anything to go by the rest of the crew had the same difficulty at getting off to sleep as I had.

I suddenly woke up, startled out of a deep sleep by a series of loud bangs that shook the aircraft. The flight deck was brilliantly lit up by the flares hanging in the night sky above us that I could see through the roof of the cockpit canopy. The flares slowly descended towards the aircraft, with sheets of flaming material falling from them, and just upstream from us came the staccato sound of machine-guns firing and the sight of long lines of tracer shells curving across the river.

Our Gunners ran to man their turrets to fight off a possible attack, although we would have been sitting ducks to any enemy fire, exposed as we were right out in the middle of the river.

After an anxious few minutes, during which we tried to decide whether to slip the moorings and taxi away in the dark out of trouble, we eventually discovered from a passing Burmese fishing boat, the crew of which very nearly got themselves blasted out of the river by our Tail Gunner when they sailed in too close in order to investigate the strange looking, dirty white fishing boat anchored in midstream, that the Fourteenth Army had finally arrived in the city, and had discovered some Japanese soldiers attempting to escape across the river after dark.

It was a sobering thought that the Japanese soldiers had probably been watching us from the river bank throughout the day and could have picked us off at any time. It would, of course, have disclosed their position, which is possibly why they did not.

The flares eventually came to a hissing end in the water just downstream of us, and the firing slowly died down. But the grey streaks of first light were already showing across the eastern sky, and further sleep was now impossible. So we made our preparations for take-off, and although we had to cut the moorings away with an axe due to the strength of the current, and negotiate a couple of bends in the river at high speed, plus a few fishing boats that happened to be in the way before we finally got airborne. We were soon safely on our way back to Akyab, leaving Rangoon and its rotting dead far behind.

Although the European war was now at an end, and massive reinforcements and supplies could be expected from that theatre, it would obviously take some considerable time to organise and to transport them out to the Far East.

In the meantime, the 'Forgotten Fourteenth', as the Fourteenth Army had become to be known, would not only have to hold the fort with the very limited supplies and manpower which was available to them at that time, but also to consolidate their already impressive gains, and continue to push the Japanese armies back across Siam and Malaya. It was obviously going to be a difficult job, because the Japanese were giving no indication, at that time, that they were going without a fight, and there was no doubt in anybody's mind about their determination to fight to the last man.

The squadron would also be taking an even more active part, now that Rangoon could be used as a forward base, as it would bring the far reaches of the Gulf of Siam and the South China seas well within our range, giving us an opportunity to cut off war supplies to the Japanese Army. At that time, it was being supplied by shipping crossing the Gulf of Siam, to Burma and Malaya. So, all in all, it looked as though we were in for a pretty interesting time of it.

Shortly after our return to Akyab, we were quietly sitting in the mess relaxing after dinner one evening, when we were all startled by a series of loud crashes and bangs, which, suddenly and without warning, reverberated loudly across the harbour, and flashes of brilliant light showed through the portholes, lighting up the cabin.

We knew that at least a division of the Japanese Army was only ten miles away from us upstream, so there was little doubt in anybody's mind that we were under attack, and that our first responsibility was to get the aircraft airborne and out of harm's way.

I dived for my Mae West and flying gear, and rushed to the side of the ship to wait for the dinghy, in order to get my pre-flight completed, and the engines started before the rest of the crew arrived. To my surprise, all the firing appeared to be coming from the warships anchored further out in the deeper water of the outer harbour, with no apparent returning enemy fire. The explanation was soon forthcoming. It appeared that the navy were celebrating VE Day by blasting off a few merry rounds into the night sky, and had quite forgotten to mention it to us.

I could have quite cheerfully got airborne at that moment, and given His Majesty's Royal Navy the benefit of the depth charges still hanging in our bomb bay. But they really did have every excuse to let off steam, as the navy had been pretty hard hit in all theatres of the Second World War. So I do not think that in the end anybody held the noisy rumpus that they made, and the near heart attacks that they caused us, against them. Indeed, I rather think that we did a bit of celebrating on our own account that night. But the memory of the rest of that evening has dimmed now, probably due to the passing of the years. It did, however, demonstrate in no uncertain way that the Far East war was not yet over, and that we still had to very much keep our guard up.

Chapter Nine

Shadowing a
Japanese Cruiser

We continued to carry out a number of fairly uneventful long range anti-shipping and anti-submarine patrols over the Indian Ocean as we waited for the move down to Syriam. Syriam was an out of use logging camp situated just up the river from Rangoon. One of the patrols also involved the shadowing of a Japanese heavy cruiser moving steadily up through the Malacca Straights towards the Andaman Islands, which were soon to be liberated by the British Navy. Constantly and accurately establishing the cruiser's position was, therefore, of the greatest importance to the success of the naval operation, and a twenty-four hour cover by flying-boats was maintained over the area to keep track of the cruiser's movements.

Of equal importance to the success of our operation, was keeping well out of the way of any Japanese fighters that might just happen to be hanging about around the Andaman Islands. We already knew that there was a fighter airfield there, which we proved, nearly to our cost on a much later sortie, when we incautiously climbed to watch Port Blair being bombarded from the sea by the Royal Navy, and got jumped by a Japanese fighter for our pains. So it was obviously going to be necessary to be very cautious on this trip.

The cruiser's approximate position was already known from previous intelligence reports. We cautiously approached its last known position, flying at sea level in order to avoid detection from their radar. When it was judged that we were just within radar range, 'Zebra' was climbed to one thousand feet, the radar was switched on for a couple of quick sweeps of the screen, which was just long enough to establish the warship's course and speed, and we then quickly descended to sea level again. We retired rapidly to a safe distance, hoping that the cruiser had not got a fix on us and was even then vectoring fighters on to our position.

The anti-submarine and anti-shipping patrol was then resumed at a safe distance, until it was time to make another check. We returned to the area of the target a number of times during the sortie, making the approach at irregular intervals, and on different headings, in order to fox the enemy, just in case he had succeeded in getting a radar fix on us during our first visit. But, fortunately for my peace of mind, we were never quite close enough for a visual sighting, and to our great relief he did not appear to have fighter cover either, or else he had been unable to get a radar fix on us. None of the crew were sorry, however, when our relief aircraft was spotted approaching on the horizon, and we were able to return to base, leaving the Royal Navy to sort out the problem in their own inimitable way. We did learn much later that the cruiser had turned for home long before reaching the Andaman Islands. So its approach to the area at that critical time must have been quite fortuitous, and not the result of prior knowledge.

'Zebra's' flying hours were now rapidly building up with the long operational sorties that we were flying in her, and she was now long overdue for a major servicing. This particular servicing could not be carried out at Akyab due to the lack of facilities there. In addition to which, the unconventional landing on the Pegu, which had strained quite a few of her underwater hull rivets, and the severe battering that her chines were taking from the heavy bomb and refuelling scows as they were banged up against her hull in the heavy swells rolling in from the Indian Ocean, meant that she was now leaking like a sieve. A lot of time was being wasted pumping out her bilges with the auxiliary power unit before take-off.

The whole crew were, therefore, delighted when we walked into the makeshift Operations Room for another early morning patrol, to see that the track shown on the Ops. Room map would take us back across the Indian Ocean to the quiet beauty of Ceylon. There we could deliver 'Zebra' into the hands of her caring ground crew for a good wash and brush up, and to pick up a new, more advanced Sunderland for the continuing battle against the Japanese in Burma. It would also give us all the opportunity to have a refreshing freshwater shower, and a good night's sleep away from the oppressive heat and noise of the three tier bunks situated in the hold of the *Manilla*, and the frenetic twenty-four hour activity of an operational squadron.

A solitary catamaran skimming lightly across the surface of the large ocean swells, and well out of the sight of land, was the first indication that we had that we were nearing Koggala. I wondered if the adventurous crew below us were my old friends, One Leg and his First Mate, because it was just the sort of thing that they would have got up to, as I already knew to my cost from the fishing trip on which I had accompanied them. I had innocently thought that I was going to spend a pleasant, relaxing day's fishing in the calm waters of the lagoon. But, that time we had finished up well out of the sight of land in a violent monsoon storm, finally streaking across an unseen reef in the lashing rain on the crest of a giant Indian Ocean breaker.

They both looked up and gave us a friendly wave, as we

roared across them at low level and were soon out of sight, lost in the immensity of the surrounding ocean.

I looked back at 'Zebra' from the dinghy as we left her for the last time. She had served us well whilst we had been together, and had staunchly stood up to the violence of the monsoon storms as we flew her through them at low level, and the inevitable hard landings made in difficult circumstances in all weathers. But she was now looking distinctly the worse for wear, with her once pristine white wings and hull streaked with oil and dirt; and she now sagged listlessly in the water from the weight of water flooding into her bilges, instead of riding proudly high as she had once done. So it was now time to give her a good rest while we waited for the arrival of the new Sunderland V, which was still in transit from England.

The Medical Officer at Koggala gave me a good check over, and then after what seemed an age he said, 'I am sorry, my lad, but I am afraid that there is nothing that I can do for you here to put you right.' My heart sank deep down into my boots. It seemed a heartless twist of fate to have survived unscathed from all the tricks that our original 'Zebras' had played upon us, and the many hours of hazardous operational flying, only to be struck down by some dreadful tropical disease.

I looked anxiously at him. But he again shook his head with the resigned air of a man about to pronounce a death sentence. He then said, 'I am afraid that the only cure for you is the cool air of the mountains, so I intend to take you off of flying for a month and send you to a holiday camp in the hills.' He grinned at my obvious relief and delight, knowing full well that he had had me going for a short while. But, decent man that he was, he fully understood that a rest away from the pressures of the Burma war for a short period would relieve the build-up of tension in the crew, as well as get us all medically fit again.

Before setting off for the hills, we spent a few relaxing nights in the aircrew club in Columbo, where the pleasures of the unfamiliar cool beer on offer, proved to be rather too much of an attraction for some of us. But eventually we set off for the hill station on a delightful little wood-burning steam train, that slowly chuffed its rather noisy way along a single track lined by dense masses of bougainvillea, which occasionally swept into the open windows, leaving the floor covered with a mass of purple blossom.

On each side of the track, spreading out into the far distance were endless low lying fields of rice paddy being tilled by Celanese farmers with pairs of slow moving oxen. Following closely behind them, were women bent almost double, who were planting handfuls of rice seedlings deep into water that had been retained on the fields by the mud dykes that had been laboriously built around them.

The countryside slowly began to change from paddy, to primary jungle, as we began the long climb into the foothills. Long lines of lianas hanging from giant trees began to replace the bouganvillea, and in an occasional clearing massive elephants could be seen using their prodigious strength to slowly move the sawn down timber.

It was a peaceful and idyllic scene, and one that was a very far cry from the murderous war that we had just left behind in Burma. The effect on the crew of the quiet peaceful atmosphere was very marked. Faces that for the last few months had been tense and drawn, began to relax, and the normal banter that always took place between crew members, even under the most difficult circumstances, became cheerful and light hearted. It had a beneficial and calming effect on everyone in the carriage.

The breeze flowing through the open windows, that had been such a welcome relief as we left the steamy heat and humidity of Columbo, was now beginning to cool down with the increasing altitude; and, although the temperature was probably still in the seventies, it was comforting to put on the jumpers that we had providentially brought with us, which had not been used since we left Ireland over a year ago. The air continued to cool down, and as we climbed higher, the jungle slowly gave way to vast vistas of tea plantations, stretching away down the terraced hillsides as far as the eye could see.

It was in this bright, clear cool air of the mountains that we finally came to the low lying bungalows of the rest camp, and the quiet privacy of individual rooms, clean sheets and, above all, the wonderful luxury of cool, refreshing, freshwater showers.

As the Medical Officer had quite rightly predicted, all the infections with which we had been plagued, in the heat and high humidity of Burma, began to quickly clear up, and the bald patches on our heads where hair had fallen out, were soon covered with hair again. But because of the unsightly sores on our legs and arms, and the bald patches on our heads, it was a cause of acute embarrassment to me, and I am sure to the rest of the crew, to find as we entered the lounge for the first time a number of young service girls on leave who had just arrived from Europe. The embarrassment, however, was short lived, as those decent girls treated us with the utmost consideration, and we were all soon on friendly terms.

Although the WAAFs that served on the Far East stations carried out a superb job which relieved many airmen for more hazardous front line duties, they were also able to show a compassion and understanding that particularly showed itself one evening in the lounge when a large log that had been blazing on the fire fell into the hearth with a loud crash that startled everybody in the room. One young gunner, who perhaps had had to face more than we should ever be called upon to do, leapt to his feet staring uncomprehendingly at the fire, and shaking uncontrollably. There was a short, embarrassed silence until one young WAAF, barely out of her teens, and with a deep compassion and understanding far beyond her years, got up and gently led him quietly from the room.

I was particularly fortunate to discover on one of my early morning walks across the hill tops, a deep pool of clear water that had been formed by large boulders damming up a mountain stream. The water was jolly cold, but enormously invigorating and refreshing; and it was pure delight to dry out on the bank afterwards in the warmth of the early morning sun, and to idly enjoy for the time the feeling of being without a care in the world, the spectacular panoramic view of the spreading tea plantations and the dark green of the jungle canopy laying far below.

The time passed all too quickly, and we were soon on our way back to Koggala, taking the very necessary precaution to sample a few cold beers in the aircrew club on the way back. We arrived back a great deal fitter and more relaxed than when we left, and we were all pronounced fit and well by the Medical Officer, and ready for operational flying once more.

The flying-boat trots were now empty of the Sunderlands and Catalinas that had filled them when we had first arrived at Koggala, as all the squadrons that had been stationed there when we first arrived were by now deployed to the war zone.

Moored up to the closest buoy, patiently waiting to be towed up the slipway for her major overhaul, was our old 'Zebra'. All her guns had been withdrawn, making her look a bit toothless, and she was still looking very miserable and down at heel. But moored alongside her was a brand new Sunderland Mk.V. She was riding high in the water, and looking very spruce and perky with her coat of new white paint shining brightly in the morning sun, and with the light ominously glinting off the oiled, black barrels of her machine-guns.

We took the new 'Zebra' up for an acceptance check at low level round the coastline. The American twin Wasp engines had been uprated, and were now giving significantly more power, which was to give us a big advantage when taking-off from the quite often narrow rivers and lakes from which we would be operating from now on. All her equipment worked well, something that we had not been used to for some time. So it was with a great deal of confidence in our new aircraft that we made preparations to return to Burma and the war zone once more.

During our stay in Ceylon, the squadron had moved to Syriam in Burma, which was an out of use logging camp, about ten miles up the river from Rangoon. We did a couple of low circuits over the area when we arrived to check it out. The river at that point was narrow and winding; and now that Rangoon was coming back to life after the occupation, it was full of small boats plying their trade, any one of which could easily rip the bottom out of a flying-boat if it hit one during take-off or landing.

Manoeuvring too would be a problem in the very restricted space available. But it was all that we had, so we would have to make the most of it and try to keep out of trouble, something that we had certainly not been very good at up to now. We spent several days preparing the aircraft for the offensive operations against enemy shipping that we would now be carrying out, mainly in the Gulf of Siam.

It was on one dark night during this period, that Ratty decided to join the crew, nearly giving me a heart attack in the process. Our initial rather innocent hope was that he would decide of his own free will that a flying-boat was not the place for him, and that he would leave of his own accord. He seemed to settle down quite happily in the dark recesses of the wing, however, where he had made his home, presumably existing on the small scraps of food that inevitably found their way into the bilges, and taking the noise of the engines, and the bouncing about in the air with complete equanimity like a seasoned traveller. He also took a strange liking for the taste of the plastic knobs mounted on top of the throttle and pitch control levers, which he progressively gnawed away when left to his own devices, finally leaving only four metal rods standing up with which to control the engines. We eventually became quite adept at handling the aircraft with half the throttle knobs missing, which was very much an acquired skill.

He also chewed up all my carefully kept Flight Engineer's logs, which were filled in at regular intervals during flight, and gave valuable information afterwards of the condition of the engines and their fuel consumption.

I remember that the Flight Engineer Leader's face was a picture when I tried to explain to him, completely without success, that I was unable to hand in my Engineer's logs because they had been eaten by our rat. I had an uneasy feeling afterwards that for some reason he did not fully believe me.

Although we had learned to cope very well without the throttle and pitch lever knobs, our main concern was that he would take a fancy to a tasty piece of electrical wiring insulation or, even worse, the plastic covering of the main fuel feeds to the engines. Every effort was, therefore, made to get rid of him, first by the crew and then by desperate attempts of the ground crew, all without avail. He was certainly a whole lot smarter than we were. We finally had to give up the unequal struggle and accept him as a permanent non-paying passenger.

As a final resort, the Co-Pilot darkly suggested that at the end of each flight we leave him out a meal of surplus flying rations, on the quite reasonable assumption that if that did not get rid of him then nothing would.

Although he quite obviously did not expect us to take his remarks seriously, we all saw some merit in the suggestion, because it was becoming increasingly obvious that Ratty was determined to stay with us whatever we thought about it, and it was important that we should try to limit any damage that he might do to the aircraft. The result was, that as I was always the first man on and the last man off the aircraft after flight, I was volunteered by all my good friends to regularly put out our surplus flying rations in the faint hope that a full stomach and a contented mind would take his mind off any ideas that he might be entertaining about our main fuel feeds.

Feeding Ratty became a daily ritual that perversely gave me a great deal of pleasure and satisfaction; and on many occasions, I would see his unblinking brown eyes viewing me anxiously from the dark safety of the wing root as I ladled out a liberal helping of stew, whilst the rest of the crew waited patiently for me in the dinghy to go ashore.

Despite the bizarre arrangement, and the endless ribbing that we had to accept from the other crews on the squadron, the system seemed to have worked well because as far as we could find out, no further damage was done to the aircraft by Ratty, and we certainly had a very contented passenger on board.

Ratty stayed for many weeks, sharing all our adventures with us with his usual unshakeable aplomb. But eventually we paid another quick visit to Ceylon, where 'Zebra' was taken up the slipway for some remedial work on her hull.

I paid an early morning visit to the beached aircraft to check on the progress of the work, and to top up Ratty's rations. As I approached the flying-boat, a small grey shape appeared at the top of the entrance ladder and hesitated there for a short time. He once again regarded me steadily with those large brown bright eyes, and then just as he had done when we first met, scurried leisurely down the ladder and disappeared for ever into the undergrowth.

The crew were delighted when I told them that he had finally gone. They were quite right, of course, as he had been an infernal nuisance and a highly dangerous one too, with his curious appetite for plastic throttle knobs. But I could not help remembering the cool courage with which he had faced me that first dark night on the Pegu, and how against all the odds he had survived the high G-forces, and the screaming crescendo of sound from the blazing guns and roaring engines as we carried out the attacks on enemy shipping in the Gulf, and when we fought off the Japanese fighter over Car Nicobar. So, despite all the worry that he had caused us in the past, and the damage that he had done to 'Zebra', I secretly wished him well in the new country that he had chosen to live in, and the rat adventures that would now befall him there. But for the time being, Ratty was still with us and fully intended to stay.

Chapter Ten

Offensive Anti-Shipping Strikes in the Gulf of Siam

All sorties from now on would have to be flown during the hours of daylight, as it would be far too dangerous to take off or land on a narrow winding river in the dark, with the ever present risk of hitting a fishing boat or partly submerged tree trunk. But the daylight hours would still give us time for an effective range of about fifteen hundred miles. This would be more than sufficient to take us well down into the Gulf of Siam where we expected to find most of our targets; and, most important of all, as far as I was concerned, sufficient fuel to get back to base again.

Despite the difficult take-off, there was no point in going on an operational sortie without a full load of bombs, fuel and ammunition. So, 'Zebra' was laying low in the water under the weight of a full load as I climbed aboard her in the dark, in readiness for our first anti-shipping offensive in the Gulf.

We waited until the first pale streaks of daylight were showing in the morning sky before starting the engines; and by the time that we had slipped our moorings, and completed the engine run up check, it was broad daylight. Fortunately for us, a fresh wind was blowing straight up the river, so that we could take-off downstream and into wind, and 'Zebra' would not have to fight her way against a strong current during the take-off run.

But not half a mile away from us was a bend in the river that we could not see round, and the short distance that we had to run before we arrived at the bend would make it difficult to get 'Zebra' up on the step with the heavy load that she was carrying before we reached it. A further complication that day, was that we did not have the luxury of a control launch that could be sent to investigate what was round the bend of the river; so there was nothing for it but to open up the taps wide, and see what happened when we got round the corner.

With the extra power available from the new uprated twin Wasp engines, 'Zebra' responded well to full throttle, and quickly came up on the step, which gave the Pilots a very limited amount of aileron and rudder control. But the suction on the bottom of the hull from the smooth surface of the water made it impossible to break the grip of the river. The result was that we arrived at the bend travelling at a good eighty knots, with both Pilots trying desperately to get her airborne by shaking the stick backwards and forwards. It was, of course, Murphy's law that there had to be something just round the bend, and so there was – a large fishing boat which was fortuitously just to the starboard of our track. I had a brief glimpse, as she flashed by under our starboard wing, of the splashes made by her crew as they jumped overboard. I remember thinking at the time that jumping overboard would not have done them a great deal of good if we had hit her square on with six tons of bombs on board, all primed and ready to go off; and it would not have done much for our life expectancy either, now that I come to think about it.

Once we had rounded the bend in the river, and levelled out, the wind was now on our beam, making 'Zebra' even more determined to stay on the water. The Pilots were using all their skill to keep both floats level and out of the river, so there was no question now of evading anything that happened to get in the way. But luck was with us, because after running for some considerable distance on the water, we eventually hit a turbulent rip current that was crossing the river almost at right angles, which fortunately broke the suction of water on our hull and propelled us unceremoniously into the air and over the tall jungle trees that lined the bank. The Navigator estimated afterwards that we had run over four miles at about ninety knots before finally lifting off. It was a trick that none of us wished to repeat, and all take-offs after that were preceded by a precautionary check with a launch.

We quickly crossed the point in the river at the centre of Rangoon where we had spent such an uncomfortable night a few months before, and headed out across the Delta of the Pegu and into the Gulf of Tavoy, flying at fifty feet and sometimes below in order to avoid detection. As soon as we had coasted out and were well clear of the fishing boats and fish traps that covered the inshore water of that area, the guns were warmed up, the turrets checked, and we were ready for action.

Eventually, we turned east and started a climb to cross the hills of central Siam. The air was cool and pleasant at altitude, and a welcome relief after the soporific heat of the jungle. But we were now over enemy held territory, and there was every possibility that there might be a fighter lurking somewhere in the high cu. through which we were intermittently passing, which kept us all very much on our toes.

Siam was safely crossed and, with the gulf now showing a shimmering silver in the distance, we commenced our let down to the comparative safety of low level flight. All the Gunners were now in their positions and alert for a possible attack from fighters; but with the exception of the beam position, which housed the big and massively powerful .5

machine-gun, they all missed the clearing in the jungle which unexpectedly flashed by just fifty feet below us. The clearing contained a large wooden hut, and a tall wooden tripod mast which was topped by an ominous looking radar aerial.

The starboard beam gun was normally manned by a fully trained air Gunner. But at that moment, one of the Wireless Operators who had never fired a gun in his life before, was being instructed in its operation by the beam Gunner. He fortunately spotted the radar station as it came into view, and with a completely reflex action squeezed the trigger of the big .5. The muzzle of the gun shot upwards, as they always did unless a very tight grip was maintained on them, with the recoil depositing the bemused Wireless Operator on the deck of the rear compartment. To our astonishment, the result was spectacular: the mast collapsed in a tangled heap and the whole hut was moved bodily sideways as though pushed by a tank, leaving it leaning drunkenly to one side. There was no doubt then in anybody's mind, that the quite remarkable quickness and accuracy of his response had prevented our position being reported to the enemy fighters. Nobody could have survived the ferocious blast of shells that had torn the hut apart. So his reputation for ever afterwards as the squadron's dead shot became unassailable.

Two quick low level orbits round the smouldering site confirmed that the radar station had been completely destroyed, and that there was no possibility of survivors being left to report our position. But things were not what they had first seemed, because shortly after the action had taken place I vacated the Flight Engineer's panel to take my turn in the front turret from the Second Engineer. As I passed through the galley I picked up a cup of coffee, and at the same time took a cup up to the Tail Gunner. He centralised his turret and opened the back doors when I banged on them, and as he did so the smell of hot gun oil and cordite fumes drifted out. The breech blocks of his four Brownings were nearly red hot to the touch. So the secret was out. It was the five thousand rounds a minute pouring out of the tail turret's guns that had so devastated the radar station. But there seemed little point in spoiling the Wireless Operator's moment of glory, so from then on we kept our secret to ourselves.

It was hot and humid again down at low level, but a refreshing blast of relatively cool air poured through the gap between the twin guns and their housings, keeping me comfortably cool. The sea flashed by only twenty feet below our keel, and from the vantage position of the front turret it was possible to clearly see the reef down through the clear blue shallow waters of the Gulf.

Large shoals of fish flashed a bright silver as they twisted and turned in the strong sunlight, and the occasional solitary streamlined figure of a shark cast a dark menacing shadow across the white coral sand of the sea bed as it glided effortlessly across it. On several occasions we had to make a quick diversion, to check out a distant disturbance on the surface of the sea, or a radar contact, only to find an innocent school of porpoises enjoying themselves in the warm water, or some floating debris.

It was on one such occasion, that out of the corner of my eye, I thought that I spotted a dark shape partially concealed behind one of the numerous Siamese fishing traps that cover the close inshore waters of the Gulf. The traps are usually constructed from long stout bamboo poles, which are driven firmly into the sea bed at close intervals to form a circle about one hundred yards across. Two other lines of poles form a funnel through which fish are carried into the circle by the incoming tide, so trapping them.

A tight turn to starboard put us on a heading for it, and as we rapidly closed the fish trap it became clear that the shadow lurking behind it was a large tank-landing craft with an unmanned machine-gun swinging idly on the stern.

The steady throbbing of 'Zebra's' engines now changed to a high pitched screaming roar as the throttles were pushed hard through the gate to give us combat power. I positioned the red, glowing ring on the gun-sight just in front of the target in order to compensate for our forward movement, whilst hoping against hope that we would get to within the twelve hundred yard range of my guns before the tank-landing craft crew got to theirs, and that I could get in the first shot at them.

Under my feet, the four fixed Brownings which were fired remotely by the First Pilot, burst into life with a loud staccato hammering noise that made me jump and momentarily loose sight of the ship. We were still clearly well out of range, and the rounds splashed harmlessly into the water well short of the target. But the sudden noise of the guns had alerted the crew of the tank-landing craft, and one man sprinted for the stern machine-gun. As he did so, I squeezed the triggers just before he got to his gun, and to my surprise he just disappeared from view. The Co-Pilot reported afterwards that he had seen him smashed bodily backwards over the side and into the sea from the ferocious blast of rounds hitting him. He must have been caught cleanly in the centre of the cone of fire. By now we had over flown the target and were banking round in a tight turn to bring the beam and mid-upper guns to bear. They all opened up simultaneously, filling 'Zebra' with the acrid smell of cordite fumes and making her shake violently from end to end. Finally, the Tail Gunner opened up as the target came into his sights, adding the shattering sound of his four Brownings to the general cacophony of noise; and yet, despite the excitement of the action and the deep concentration required to keep the target firmly within the red circle of the gunsight, I could not help sparing a quick thought for Ratty who was sheltering far out in the darkness of the wing, enveloped in the deafening noise of the guns and engines, and no doubt wondering what on earth was going on.

We levelled out and headed away from the target, ready to turn in for a low level bombing run. The bomb doors opened with a crash, and the bomb cradles holding their deadly cargo trundled out under the wings. But as we started the run in to the target, it became obvious that the tank-landing craft was in dire trouble. Although it was still under way, the course was unsteady, and its bows eventually became firmly stuck in the fishing trap that had originally sheltered it, with its propellers churning uselessly in the water.

As neither the tank-landing craft, which had been holed in several places by our heavy .5s, nor the motionless distorted figures laying on her deck, were now likely to be of any further use to the enemy, we retracted the bomb racks, and continued on our way down the Gulf, saving our weapons for the next target.

It turned out to be a wise decision, because our saved weapons were to be successfully used against a further target later in the sortie, and the tank-landing craft was seen many days later by a patrolling squadron aircraft on the 'Milk run' still stuck firmly in the fishing trap.

The area of the Gulf that we were now patrolling was dotted with small, mainly uninhabited islands, although occasionally a solitary fisherman's hut could be seen on the only strip of white coral sand that was not covered with dense vegetation. The islands were far too numerous for us to be able to investigate them individually. But as we passed close to one, the Mid-Upper Gunner reported seeing a flash of light, which could possibly be a reflection from perhaps a glass window or a pair of binoculars, coming from the direction of a cove that was sheltered by an overhanging cliff, and therefore in deep shadow. We cautiously circled the island, well out of the possible range of fire, ready to bank away in a hurry if necessary; but nothing was seen, so we prepared to resume the patrol. Just as we were heading away, however, the Tail Gunner reported seeing another flash from roughly the same position. So once again we circled the island, and this time we spotted it: a small coaster that had been carefully camouflaged with masses of large coconut fronds and other tropical vegetation. It was obvious from the trouble that had been taken to hide the vessel that it was of some strategic importance; but because of the overhanging cliff and dense vegetation it was impossible to bomb it from above, and our depth charges were set to detonate at too great a depth to activate in the shallow water. So we closed the target, raking the vessel with a mass of machine-gun fire from all the guns that could be brought to bear as we passed her beam, and then we tried a new trick that was to serve us well on later sorties.

'Zebra' was climbed steadily to about five thousand feet, and then, with the throttles wide open and bombs selected, we turned and dived down to sea level, gaining as much speed from the dive as we could, and releasing the two, two hundred and fifty pound anti-submarine bombs just before reaching the target at about two hundred knots.

The bombs skipped across the surface of the water like a stone thrown across the surface of a pond, leaving a series of rings of disturbed water where they had ricocheted off the surface of the sea. Both were heading straight for the side of the vessel when we lost sight of them, as with the control columns hard back in the Pilots' stomachs we shot over the cliff face with only feet to spare.

To the crew's intense annoyance both bombs failed to explode. So once again 'Zebra' was climbed to height, and made a second, fast heart-stopping run in. Again the second lot of bombs failed to explode. But a slow low level run past the vessel afterwards showed at least two gaping ragged holes in her side where the bombs had entered, and her wooden superstructure was shattered beyond repair. This would obviously put her out of commission, if not permanently at least for a very long time to come. So, once again, 'Zebra's' engines were throttled back to cruising power, and we continued our patrol along the Gulf.

On debriefing back at base, the armament officer concluded that due to the low height of the attack, the wind-driven propellers that armed the bombs, after they had left the aircraft, had had insufficient time to wind down far enough to release the firing pins. The travel of the arming propellers was accordingly adjusted for future sorties, nearly blowing the tail off of the next aircraft that tried it. But even when they got the timing right, the explosion would give the aircraft a firm kick from behind to assist it on its way, and would also have probably given the rear turret perspex a good wash into the bargain.

Time was now getting short if we were to get 'Zebra' back to the Pegu and bedded down before darkness fell, and I was already beginning to eye my fuel gauges with some concern. We headed for the coast and the general direction of a black speck in the distance that was roughly on our track.

As we neared the new target, it became clear that it was a small wooden coaster, which was towing a very large open-topped sampan lashed to its side. They both looked innocent enough from a distance and we almost passed them by without making an attack. But when we over-flew them, we discovered that the sampan was full of large lorry tyres, which would be an invaluable cargo for the Japanese Army if it got through, and thoroughly well worth destroying.

This time there was plenty of depth of water to activate the depth charges, which in any case was all that was left in the bomb bay. So, we turned back towards the target and made preparations for a slow run in, aiming to drop the weapons one each side of the vessels. This was just the type of attack that would normally be carried out against a submarine, with the object of crushing the pressure hull between the two explosions. But as we were now to find out, it was equally as effective against small boats.

For this type of attack, a long, slow run in was required in order to line the aircraft up accurately with the vessel's beam. So the bombing run was made from a range of about five miles, with bomb doors open and weapons selected ready for release by the First Pilot, and with all the Gunners very much on the alert for answering fire from the target. For good measure, I also sprayed the target from the nose turret with the twin VGOs, as soon as it came within range.

The depth charges fell tumbling from the bomb racks, just before we over-flew the targets, and almost immediately afterwards there was a report from the Tail Gunner. 'Fifty-fifty, no line error' as they splashed into the sea, which indicated that they had been accurately placed in the water each side of the two vessels.

There was a short anxious delay as the depth charges sank to the depth at which they would detonate, and then suddenly a violent shock wave covered the calm blue surface of the sea, leaving the surface of the water boiling and blackened by the residue from the explosions. This was immediately followed by two towering columns of water which completely hid the targets from view as the water and spray cascaded down.

By the time that we had banked round and levelled out, it was clear that both vessels had been completely shattered by the force of the combined blasts, and that what little remained of them was floating on the surface of the sea, surrounded by a mass of floating debris and lorry tyres.

We slowly circled the wreckage several times, searching for any possible survivors, as the sea was calm enough for us to have landed and picked them up if any had been spotted. But, realistically, there was very little hope that anybody could have survived the crushing blast of the two depth charges, or the sharks that would have immediately been attracted to the area by the smell of blood. So we resumed our original heading for the coast, only making a slight diversion from track to investigate a sailing boat in the distance which was carrying a large brown sail.

The sailing boat turned out to be a large sampan under full sail, which was heading directly for the coastline of Malaya, now just visible on the horizon. It was impossible to see her cargo from the air because it was all concealed below the decking, with the exception of a small camouflaged army vehicle that was firmly lashed down near the stern. It was obvious from the military vehicle that she was almost certainly carrying strategic supplies of some sort, and that we ought to do something about it if we could.

Our bomb bay was now completely empty of all the bombs and depth charges, with which we had left Burma, and we only had sufficient ammunition left to defend ourselves in the event of a fighter attack on the way back to base. Despite the shortage of weapons, however, it was decided that the least we could do was to give her crew a good fright, and make them think twice about future trips.

'Zebra' was climbed to about two thousand feet and then cranked round really hard in a tight turning dive, with all her four engines roaring under full combat power, and the superchargers screaming like four demented banshees. We dived low over the boat at mast top height, pulling hard back on the stick as we roared across her, and missing the top of her sail by a few feet. The very high G-forces generated by the tight turn away from the vessel had made it difficult to turn the head in order to keep the target in view, but once we had levelled out she came into sight just in front of our nose. The effect of the manoeuvre on the sampan, had been as astonishing as it had been unexpected, because the force generated by our four slipstreams had filled her sail and had quite literally blown her over almost level with the surface of the sea, and she was only then beginning to slowly right herself with the masses of sea water pouring from her deck carrying away the debris of her rigging.

The military vehicle, which had been lashed near the stern, had broken away from its securing ropes and disappeared over the side. It was also highly likely that there would have been a good deal of chaos and damage inside the vessel. So, operational experience taught us another trick with the flying-boat that day for which we had not been trained, and which her designer almost certainly had not thought of.

Following squadron crews used the idea when they were running short of bombs and ammunition, but with only a moderate degree of success because the crafty Japanese sailors quickly became aware of what was going on, and would always lower the sails at the approach of an aircraft, so defeating the object of the exercise. We also felt that the Japanese became very unsporting by heavily arming innocent-looking sailing vessels with concealed guns, rather like the 'Q' ships of World War One. This had unfortunate results for more than one of our aircraft, although the Japanese often got more than they bargained for if they were unfortunate enough to run up against a fully armed Sunderland.

Once again, we turned and headed for the coast, leaving the sailing boat wallowing heavily from side to side in the still heaving water, and with one crew member who had just emerged through a hatch from below shaking his fist in defiance at us. He, at least, didn't seem to be at all intimidated by all the damage that we had caused to his vessel, although it may very well have been bravado on his part. We were sorely tempted to give him another sharp lesson in good manners, but time was now pressing, so we continued on our way, well satisfied that we had done as much damage as we possibly could under the circumstances.

We crossed the coast of Siam with the creamy white sand of the beach flashing by just a few feet beneath our keel in a low level attempt to avoid detection by enemy radar, and were soon passing above the massive trees of the Siamese primary jungle.

A long dark swathe cut through the trees which was showing in the distance and stretching as far as the eye could see from side to side, proved to be the cutting for a railway line, with the metal rails glinting brightly in the sunshine as we passed across them.

It was the 'Death Railway', as it had come to be generally known, because of the thousands of unfortunate Allied prisoners of war who had lost their lives from disease, malnutrition and ill-treatment, and had been forced to live in abject misery by their captors whilst building it.

We banked sharply round and followed the gleaming steel lines northwards. Following the railway would not take us far out of our way, and the slight diversion would be very well worth while if it brought some ray of hope to any Allied prisoners of war who might happen to spot the red, white and blue rondels on 'Zebra's' flanks.

Our fuel state eventually forced us to leave the railway and climb up over the hills of central Siam on our way to the Indian Ocean. There had been no sign of life on the railway, but we found out afterwards that the Japanese guards would force their prisoners under the concealment of the forest canopy whenever an aircraft was heard approaching. It was very possible, therefore, that the slight extra risk that we had taken in making the diversion from track, had been worthwhile if we had been spotted by any of the prisoners.

The narrow neck of Siam was quickly crossed and we headed out across the Indian Ocean, keeping a sharp look out for Japanese submarines travelling on the surface, or Japanese shipping which could be reported when we got back to base.

There was now a short time to relax, before we arrived within range of the Japanese fighters operating out of the Andaman Islands; and before long the welcome roar of the galley Primuses and the smell of stew, which was the 'Boat' man's staple diet, wafted up the companion way to the flight deck. But foolishly, we were to relax for just a little too long.

The long, low coastline of Car Nicobar slowly began to detach itself from the low cloud on the horizon, as we approached the islands, and continuous bright flashes of light and great columns of dense billowing black smoke showed from the area surrounding Port Blair in the distance. We already knew from our briefing before leaving the *Manilla*, that the Allied ships were to bombard the port that day in preparation to retake the Islands.

Although we took the wise precaution of keeping well out of the way of the Navy's guns, we did, however, climb incautiously to just below the cloud base in order to better see what was going on. It nearly proved to be the last thing that we would ever do.

As we levelled out and throttled back to cruising power, there was a click on the intercom as a microphone was switched on, and then there came a loud rush of noise and a crackling of static that could only come from the Tail Gunner's position. The sound sent a cold chill down my spine, as over the intercom came an excited shout from the normally phlegmatic Tail Gunner, 'Fighter, fighter, four o'clock high, climbing turn to starboard go, go, go.'

'Zebra' lurched forward as the four throttles were slammed through the gate and the Pilots cranked her hard round in a tight climbing turn to starboard. The high G-forces forced me hard back in my seat, but I could just see out of the corner of my eye the flashes from his guns as the fighter opened fire, and was just dimly aware in all the excitement of the staccato hammering of our guns as all the gunners brought their guns to bear on the target.

Quite contrary to what we had been told during training, the fighter pilot appeared to be quite unaffected by the high G-forces that were generated by the tight turn that we had forced on him by our turn and climb into his attack, and he stayed grimly, and it must be said very courageously on our tail, despite the massive hail of shells confronting him. Eventually, however, we providentially climbed up into the cover provided by the low cloud under which we had been previously cruising, and into which we now made our escape.

The respite gave us a chance to get the dangerously overheating engines throttled back to cruising power, before they became cooked by the high temperatures induced by the maximum power settings and supercharger pressures.

All our guns were now silent, with every round of ammunition exhausted. So, we made full use of the thin cloud cover available, carefully skirting clear patches of sky and keeping 'Zebra' twitching in the turbulence generated by the denser cloud.

It was an anxious few minutes for everybody as we cleared the area, because we were now completely defenceless against further attacks. But apart from a few small holes through the top of the hull, and well above the water-line, we had come out of it relatively unscathed, and fortunately without injury to any of the crew.

Perhaps not too surprisingly, we had by now lost all interest in the show at Port Blair, so we continued on our way back to the Pegu, as rapidly as our depleted fuel state would allow. It was, however, another lesson that we had learned the hard way that day, and that was to never drop your guard for a second, however safe the situation might appear to be. We certainly did not make the same mistake again.

The Japanese fighter which had followed us into and then lost us in the cloud cover, appeared to be quite undamaged when he was last seen by the Tail Gunner, peeling away and apparently breaking off the attack. But it was very unlikely that he could have escaped unscathed from the massive amount of fire power that we were able to bring to bear on him, which is probably why he did not press home his attack any further.

The cloud cover thickened as we approached the Pegu Delta, and we were soon bumping along in eight-eighths cloud, with only very occasional glimpses of the sea; but the end of the sortie was now in sight, and the whole crew were looking forward to a shower, even a salt water one, and a good night's sleep.

But the day was not quite over yet for the crew of 'Z' for 'Zebra', because suddenly, there was an intense flash which momentarily blinded me and a loud bang immediately below our port wing. The aircraft veered violently to starboard and lost a good deal of height before she could be brought back under control.

The loss of height took us below the cloud base where the reason for the explosion immediately became obvious. We had unknowingly over flown a large cruiser, which had been concealed from us by the low cloud, and it had fired off a warning shot, which had come a lot too close for comfort.

Fortunately for us, the aircraft was immediately identified by the ship's crew as we dropped out of the cloud on the point of the stall, so we were able to finally coast safely in across the Delta, still in one piece, but well shaken up by the very near miss. A check on our IFF transponder when we got back to base, which had been switched on just prior to the incident, showed that it was serviceable. So there was no explanation for the mistaken identification by the warship. But it was a normal hazard faced by all maritime crews. Ships quite rightly could not always wait for a positive identification before opening fire.

The tropical night was rapidly closing in as we landed and taxied up to our moorings on the Pegu; and by the time that we had moored up and shut down the four twin Wasps, we were each cocooned by twelve hours of deafening noise and vibration in a velvety black silence. But as our hearing slowly became accustomed to the quiet, the sounds of the river and the creaking of the big hull as it swung on its moorings could be heard once again, and life began to return to normality after the excitement and drama of the day.

I made a final check round the cockpit and the moorings, and then ladled out a generous portion of Ratty's stew, in spite of the fact that I was sure that he could not possibly have survived the heat and noise out in the wing during the attacks that we had made during the flight. But as I hesitated for a moment at the bow door before jumping into the waiting dinghy, a soft familiar scuffling sound came from the direction of the bomb bay. He was obviously already running down a jettison pipe, as large as life, on the way to his dinner. Quite extraordinarily, at that moment in time I felt a sense of great relief that after all the day's savage killings at least that courageous little devil was still alive and well.

We had used 'Zebra's' awesome power to the full during that operation, and the mission had been very successful in denying the Japanese Army some badly needed supplies. But I could not help remembering the twisted motionless bodies and the bloody mangled corpse that was floating face downwards in the water beside the tank-landing craft that I had shattered with my guns that day. So, although we all knew that we would have been treated with the utmost brutality, and probably executed if we had been shot down and captured, and that I should feel no pity for men who could carry out such actions, I did fervently wish that none of the killing had been necessary. It was a very subdued airman who finally climbed wearily into his bunk late that night, to fall into a deep troubled sleep, from which he awoke in the early hours of the morning, crouching fearfully by the side of the bed, bathed in sweat and shaking uncontrollably from the fear of some dreadful unknown terror.

The squadron continued with its offensive operations in the Gulf of Siam, and its aircraft penetrated even further east into the South China Sea than we had done; and in a few instances its aircraft were used in the straight bomber role against strategic targets in North Malayan ports which were out of the range of the bomber fleet, who were still confined to airfields near the Indian border.

The bomber role was a potentially very hazardous one for a large, slow-flying aircraft, such as the Sunderland flying-boat. But the very low level nature of the attacks, where the crews were quite often able to use the hilly jungle covered terrain as cover on the approach to the target, created an element of surprise which more often than not caught the Japanese defences, who were not used to enemy aircraft penetrating as far east, by complete surprise. All our aircraft returned safely from these missions, apart from a few small holes ventilating the hull, and fortunately without injury to the crew.

During this phase of the battle, the Catalina flying-boat

squadrons, with their greater endurance than the Sunderland, were often used to drop, and recover, saboteurs on the mainland of Indo-China. This was another particularly hazardous mission, successfully performed by the flying-boats in the Far East.

As the Japanese were pushed steadily back down the Malay Peninsular by the Fourteenth Army, airfields gradually became available to the Allied fighter, bomber, and transport crews, which resulted in almost total air superiority over the region. This made the boat squadrons far less isolated and exposed than they had been in their forward bases on the rivers, which were often hundreds of miles beyond the protective range of the Allied fighters.

Eventually, the squadron was withdrawn back from Burma to Ceylon, having very successfully fulfilled all its commitments in the Gulf, by effectively cutting off war supplies to the Japanese Army in Malaya.

Chapter Eleven

Preparations for 'Operation Zipper': The War Ends

The move to Ceylon gave the squadron servicing crews an opportunity to get the aircraft right up to operational fighting readiness again in preparation for 'Operation Zipper', which was to be the retaking of Singapore. It also gave the aircrew a much needed respite from the inevitable tensions induced by operational flying.

There was little doubt in everybody's mind, at this point of the war, that the Japanese, who were now caught like rats in a trap, would fight to the last man. Nobody doubted their courage for a second. It was very obvious, therefore, that this next operation was going to be a pretty lively affair, and with all the preparations that were under way on the squadron, we were undoubtedly destined for a front seat.

But for the time being, anyhow, we were able to settle down to the occasional anti-shipping, and anti-submarine patrol, over the Indian Ocean, with a routine of radar and gunnery exercises, and with plenty of time off to relax, swimming in the gentle warmth of the Indian Ocean and visiting the local area. Also by now, WAAFs had joined some of the Far East stations, a point that was not over-looked by the returning crews, and several lasting romantic liaisons were formed on the squadron.

Ratty had left us some time before and was no doubt by

now enjoying new rat adventures, if I knew anything about him. So, my early morning stroll to catch a dinghy in order to ladle out his breakfast and to make a check on the security of the aircraft became unnecessary. But I had come to enjoy the peace and quiet of the early morning, so the mess was deserted when I arrived early for breakfast one day.

On a table in the entrance to the mess was a pile of the morning papers, and a headline in the *Straights Times* immediately caught my eye. A large bomb had been dropped by the Americans on a Japanese city that I had never heard of, completely demolishing it and killing many thousands of people. It was obvious to me even at that early stage that no nation on earth could withstand that sort of onslaught, and that there was now a real chance that the war would soon be over.

The news, however, was only accepted with some degree of caution by everybody on the squadron, as nobody dared hope that the end was really in sight, and that there was now a chance of surviving the war and returning home to wives and families. But when the second atomic bomb was detonated above Nagasaki, we all then knew that it had to be only a matter of time before the war finally came to an end.

Shortly after the dropping of the atomic bombs, the wonderful news came that Japan had finally capitulated unconditionally. It was, quite naturally, greeted with wild excitement by most people, sending one man almost berserk in the mess, where he nearly succeeded, where the whole of the Japanese Imperial army had failed, to write off half the squadron personnel by firing his revolver at random round the lounge until he was overpowered and incarcerated in the cooler for a few hours to settle down. Other exploits in the mess that night were scarcely less colourful.

But strangely enough, for reasons which were only known to themselves and which can now only be guessed at, not everyone accepted the wonderful news with the same degree of delight. Indeed, the effect on one man was so traumatic that it eventually caused him to take an action resulting in the most dreadful tragedy, which was to cause the deaths of nearly fifty people, some of whom had already suffered terribly for years as prisoners of war at the hands of the Japanese.

It was also a tragedy in which I was to take a quite innocent part; and, although it would have been quite impossible for me to have foreseen it, I have none the less ever since felt a depressing degree of guilt for what happened. But more of that later.

The delight and euphoria felt by most people that the atomic weapons dropped over Nagasaki and Hiroshima had caused Japan to finally capitulate, and that World War Two was now over for good, tended to make them indifferent to the fact that thousands of human beings had been killed and injured in those two cities. Most of the victims were women and children who were quite innocent of any of the crimes against humanity of which the Japanese servicemen were guilty.

There were many reasonable excuses for their apparent indifference, of course, as the dropping of the two bombs, although they caused the death and injury of so many thousands of people, had also, by bringing the war to an end, certainly saved the lives of hundreds of thousands of others, including Japanese lives, and possibly even including my own. We also had no knowledge then of the dreadful continuing after-effects of radiation poisoning, and, of course, in many of the great cities of Europe bomber air raids, even with conventional weapons, had killed and injured just as many people.

But despite the strong arguments in favour of using the

weapons, I always felt uneasy and unsure for many years afterwards about the morality of dropping those awful bombs on mainly innocent people, particularly as the Far East war at that time was nearly over.

One day, however, many years later, I was standing with the rest of the crew on the dispersal of an airfield situated on a small island in the middle of the Pacific Ocean. We had just returned in a Shackleton maritime aircraft from a fifteen hour search of the surrounding sea for any shipping which may have wandered into the area. The weather was pleasantly warm, with a gentle breeze tempering the heat of the late morning tropical sun. In the distance the big Pacific breakers could be heard rolling in across the reef and swirling across the placid surface of the lagoon to finish in a swirl of white coral sand on the beach, and surrounding the verges of the airfield were the graceful curving trunks of coconut trees, each surmounted by a mass of gently waving palm fronds.

It was in this place of a quiet and exquisite beauty that lulled the senses, with both my hands covering my tightly closed eyes, and with the harsh rasping voice of the bomb aimer echoing through my head that was being relayed to us through the loudspeakers situated round the dispersal from the nuclear bomber circling thousands of feet above our heads, that I distinctly saw through a blood-red haze the outline of the skeleton of my hands, from the intensity of the flash; and then felt the tearing, searing heat on the back of my neck and bare knees as an atomic bomb exploded on the tip of the island behind us.

A few seconds later the sound of the explosion reached us, quickly followed by the over-pressure, which doubled the palm trees surrounding the dispersal right over as though they had been bent by the force of a violent hurricane. Surprisingly, the sound of the explosion was quite unlike the deafening blast of sound from the large German bombs and land mines that I had experienced when at home on leave in London during the Blitz, but more like the overwhelming crack of a very loud rifle shot.

After a wait of one minute, and completely numbed by the shocking experience, we turned to look at the explosion. The atomic cloud which was already many thousands of feet high, was silhouetted against the deep azure blue of the tropical sky, with the now familiar anvil shape already forming at the top.

Tongues of brilliantly coloured flame, many thousands of feet long, flared from the sides of the boiling mass of radioactive dust smoke and steam, and in the distance could be heard the screaming cries of injured and blinded sea-birds, trying to escape, without hope, from that dreadful scene.

In five long years of war, I had often experienced fear and the degrading sense of humiliation that comes with fear when under fire. But nothing that had gone before could have prepared me for the malignant evil horror that I witnessed that day. It was then, in the light of that experience, that I knew that, all those years before, we had been wrong to both sanction and take part in the dropping of those dreadful weapons.

Once again, we left Koggala, fully loaded with spares and servicing personnel. But this time we were heading for Singapore to take over from the Japanese occupiers. Our bombs and depth charges were being left behind, as hopefully there would be no further use for them. Although, as a precaution against some maverick Japanese fighter pilot deciding to carry on the war all on his own, our guns were still loaded with their long lines of ammunition, and all the turrets were continuously manned.

The drier air of the North-East monsoon had cleared away the steamy mist normally rising from the jungle to which we had become so accustomed during the preceding few months, and the Johore Straights and Singapore Island were bathed in bright sunlight as we banked round over the great swamp of the Mandai, to land at the Royal Air Force pre-war flying-boat base, Seletar, in Singapore. It was situated on the Johore Straights coastline facing Malaya.

Not unnaturally, the camp was in a shocking mess from the hurried evacuation of the Japanese Air Force personnel. But the Japanese prisoners of war were already hard at work, clearing up the piles of rubbish, monitored by their officers who treated their own men with the utmost brutality, quite often punishing them for the slightest mistake or imagined transgression with a hard blow round the head. Such an action would have immediately resulted in a court martial for a British officer.

Their arrogant bullying and dictatorial air contrasted sharply with the attitude shown to the prisoners by British servicemen who, although not treating them with undue kindness, nevertheless behaved correctly towards a defeated enemy, despite having every good reason to hate them.

In one such instance of bullying, I ordered a Japanese officer to have a heavy crate moved. One of the two soldiers carrying the crate accidentally stumbled on the edge of a deep monsoon ditch, into which he slipped, badly tearing his shoulder on the sharp edge of the crate as he did so, and obviously sustaining severe concussion. The immediate reaction of the Japanese officer was to strike the unfortunate man several times round the head with as much force as he could as punishment for what was very obviously an accident; and it was left to me to see that the man was properly treated and cared for in the sick bay afterwards, otherwise he would almost certainly have been left to suffer on his own.

Compared with the Catalina flying-boat squadrons, the Sunderlands now became busier than ever before, because the size of their great hull and the lifting capacity of the four twin Wasp engines enabled the aircraft to be quickly changed, from an effective attack aircraft, to one suitable for passenger and freight carrying, or search and rescue missions. Sadly, quite a few still had to be flown.

One of our first flying tasks on arrival in Singapore was the search for a missing American Liberator which had disappeared somewhere over Sumatra. It took us backwards and forwards over the equator fifteen times that day, as we carried out a meticulous search of the area in which the aircraft had supposedly gone down. But nothing could be seen through the dense dark green canopy of jungle trees, and there had been very little hope of finding the crew alive from the start of the operation.

We also spent many long painstaking hours searching for other aircraft, mainly Mosquito fighters, whose unusual construction of glued together laminated wood was very susceptible to corrosion in the steamy heat of the tropics. That may well have been the reason for their disappearance.

I witnessed the complete disintegration of a Mosquito fighter-bomber, whose Pilot was attempting to celebrate the victory over the Japanese with a barrel roll over Seletar, when one wing broke away from the fuselage and he spiralled down into the Mandai. It was very sad to witness the unnecessary deaths of two brave men, especially as the dangers of war that they had previously faced with such courage had only just ended.

The aircraft was now lightened as much as possible in order to enable her to carry the maximum load of freight or passengers by removing the rest of its armament and pyrotechnics, apart from a few flame and smoke floats, which were necessary for navigation purposes; and some cane chairs were securely lashed down, mainly in the tail section, in order to accommodate our passengers in reason-able comfort. It was not Imperial Airways by a long way, but it was the best that we could do under the circumstances, and there were certainly no complaints from the passengers that we carried. Most of the passengers were Dutch people from Indonesia who had been held by the Japanese in the most appalling conditions during the war years and were only too happy to be supplied with any form of transport that would finally take them on their way home.

We flew the first passengers back to Redhills Lake, which is just outside of Madras in India, from where they could continue their journey home to Holland. They all required assistance with walking, and were only able to climb into the aircraft from the dinghy with the greatest difficulty.

Their large, luminous eyes, which were sunk back deeply into thin haggard faces, and their emaciated frames, paid eloquent and telling testimony to the awful suffering that they had endured at the hands of their captors. If anything had been needed, the sight of those poor frail women confirmed to us the awful evil against which we had been fighting for so long; and, perhaps, in some small way, it also helped to justify the loss of our comrades that we had suffered as a consequence.

The long eleven hour journey to India must have been agony for our passengers in their weakened condition because the interior of the wartime military Sunderland was completely devoid of frills. There was no sound covering over the thin aluminium skin, and the interior supporting ribs and inter-costals; so, the continuous roar and vibration from the twin Wasp engines and the constant rush of noise from the four slipstreams was deafening, and our low transit altitude meant that we always caught the worst of the turbulence from the weather. But there was not one word or murmur of complaint from those brave people; just a few quiet, grateful thanks as they were carefully assisted into the waiting dinghy when they left the aircraft at the end of the flight.

On the return journey to Singapore, we were tasked to drop off some passengers at Penang. The resulting diversion to the island, and the extra landing and take-off, used up much more fuel than had been planned for. But I was confidently assured, before we left India, that adequate refuelling facilities were waiting for us at Penang, although I wasn't all that convinced by the assurance, I must say.

The refuelling expert turned out to be an elderly Malay well past his prime who had last refuelled an Imperial Airways flying-boat well before the war. He led me to his refueller, of which he was inordinately proud. He reminded me a little of the Russian Oil Company's *Ivan*, at Habbaniya, the deck of whose refuelling scow I had so neatly perforated with one of 'Zebra's' engines. It now seemed a lifetime ago.

The refueller turned out to be a rusty five hundred gallon fuel tank which was wedged firmly inside the hull of an old metal ship's lifeboat. I eyed the unlikely contraption with a good deal of suspicion. But after the crash at Oban due to sea water finding its way into our fuel tanks, I had always carried some litmus paste with me in order to make an independent check on the condition of the fuel before each flight, and I invariably refuelled through a leather filter which effectively removed any water that might be present in the refueller's tank. I carefully checked the partly empty tank and, finding it reasonably free of water, decided that in the morning I would chance refuelling from it. In any case, we only needed a top up of fuel, and that I could confine to one fuel tank, which could be kept in reserve, and hopefully would not be necessary to use. It was either that or wait for fuel to be sent from Singapore, which could take weeks in the present state of the chaos that existed there.

I arrived at the jetty early the following morning in order to refuel the aircraft before the rest of the crew

arrived, only to find that the previous evening's disturbance, when I had checked the fuel state, had been too
much for the old lifeboat. It had finally given up the ghost
and was now resting on the bottom of the harbour, leaving
the partly empty fuel tank floating on the surface of the
water, and still lashed to the jetty.

Well, there was nothing for it. We needed the fuel badly.
The old tank was slowly towed out to the aircraft, where we
pumped as much fuel out of it with a hand pump as we
dared before it turned turtle. It was just sufficient to get us
back to Singapore, with a reasonable reserve of fuel.

That episode was a good example of how extreme meas-
ures often had to be taken to keep the Far East flying-boats
airborne under difficult circumstances. I must say that I
felt, as I sadly said goodbye to the old Malay whose
refueller I had just wrecked, that I was destined to go
through the rest of my life quite innocently destroying
other people's much loved refuelling scows.

We arrived back at Singapore feeling dog-tired and ready
for a good night's sleep, only to find that all the squadron
aircraft had been deployed on other duties, and that in our
absence we had been elected for search and rescue standby.
This duty involved the crew sleeping in the control tower,
in readiness for a quick run to the waiting dinghy should it
become necessary.

Being tired from the long flights to India and back, I
went to bed early and quickly fell into a deep, sound sleep,
quite oblivious of the bizarre and terrible event that was to
unfold that night, and in which I was to become quite
innocently involved.

I slowly became conscious of being shaken gently by the
shoulder, and when I looked up a figure was standing by
my bedside outlined by the light of a single bare bulb
hanging in the middle of the room. It was one of the
squadron Flight Engineers who I knew well. He bent down

and asked me in a whisper, so as not to disturb the other crew members, if I would take his place on the aircraft which was taking another lot of ex-prisoners to India, whilst he took over my search and rescue standby.

It was a highly unusual request, because we only normally flew with our own crews. My immediate thought was that he was not feeling well, in which case I would have been quite prepared to go. But although he said that he felt fine, he was most insistent that I should take his place on the aircraft, and could not offer any reasonable explanation why I should take his place. Eventually, however, he could see that unless he could come up with a very good reason for not flying himself, I was going back to sleep, and I told him so in no uncertain terms.

The last thing that he said to me as he turned away to leave was, 'We are going to get the chop tonight, Reg.' Although he appeared to say it very seriously, and his face was grave, it was too bizarre a statement, coming from a man who had spent the last two years facing the hazards of operational flying without losing his nerve, to be taken at all seriously. I just laughed, foolishly thinking that it was a jocular attempt to make me change my mind, and I then fell back into a deep sound sleep once more. It was an action that I have deeply regretted ever since.

Once again, I woke up with somebody shaking me by the shoulder. But this time a voice said, 'Wakey, wakey, sir, S and R call out.' It was broad daylight, and the morning was well advanced, as I quickly dressed and dashed for the waiting dinghy.

'Zebra' was rapidly coming to life as I dropped back through the hatch on to the flight deck after completing the pre-flight check on the wings. Both Pilots were strapping themselves into their seats, and the Signaller and Radar Operator were warming up their equipment. The Navigator was concentrating on his charts, and right up in the nose of the aircraft, one of the Gunners had the front turret wound back and was securing the aircraft to the buoy with the short slip in readiness for a quick release when the engines started.

Having a few moments to spare before I primed up the engines, I leaned across to the Navigator's desk to look at his chart. Our track, which had already been plotted, took us across the southern tip of Malaya into the Malacca Straights, and then across the Indian Ocean, almost as far as Car Nicobar, before returning to Singapore.

Although I feared that I already knew the answer, I said to the Navigator: 'What are we after today, Nav.?'

He replied, '"X" has failed to report in, and there is some worry that she may have gone down somewhere; so we are going to have a look round just as a precaution.' It was confirmation of my worst fears, although even then I hoped against hope that we would find them safe and well, and that the problem was just the simple failure of a wireless transmitter.

Within twenty minutes of the call out, we were cutting a clean straight line across the Johore Straights, and flying at low level across the Malayan jungle only gaining altitude to cross the foothills of the Cameron Highlands, before letting down again to fly at one thousand feet, which was our optimum search height, across the Mallacca Straights.

The long, low shoreline of Sumatra slowly became visible to the south, outlined by the whiteness of the beaches and the dark green of the jungle canopy; and dead ahead, laying right across our path, and stretching out as far as the eye could see on either side, was an ominous surging mass of black cumulonimbus cloud which was boiling up thousands of feet into the sky. The sea, at its leading edge, whipped into a frenzy of white foam due to the force of the winds generated inside the hurricane. I glanced enquiringly at the Captain, who just shrugged his shoulders by way of reply. I knew what he meant. Under the circumstances, we had to press on, come what may. But it certainly looked as though we were in for a pretty lively time of it.

'Zebra' began to feel the effects of the turbulence from the storm just before we entered it, with her wing-tips bending up and down and her tail veering from side to side as we hit the savage gusts. The rain began to splatter across the windscreen in large drops, but as soon as we entered the cloud it became a continuous pouring torrent, which rendered the windscreen wipers useless, and made it impossible to see through the glass. The top surface of the wings began to look as though we were in a wind tunnel because of the massive deluge of water which was diverted by the aerofoil shape across it.

As we penetrated further into the blackness of the clouds, the turbulence became increasingly violent, making 'Zebra' shudder and jolt in the intensity of the squalls, and sending pots and pans in the galley flying, as well as making it impossible to stand up or move about. The static dispensers on the wing-tips were quite unable to disperse the massive build-up of static electricity from which the aircraft had become so heavily charged. This resulted in the propellers looking like four giant catherine wheels as the brilliantly coloured static played in circles around their blades. It was a very dramatic illustration of the phenomenon of 'St Elmo's Fire', which had so overawed the old mariners when they saw the bright patterns of light playing round their masts and rigging during an electrical storm.

I really began to think at that stage, that 'Zebra', tough as she was, could not stand very much more of that sort of pounding. But by letting the old girl have her head, and by using the very minimum of control in order to maintain height, she held stoutly together, and we eventually emerged into the dead calm eye of the storm.

The storm centre was surrounded by a circle of boiling

storm clouds, perhaps ten miles across, which looked rather like a giant shimmering amphitheatre. The now calm sea beneath it was being brilliantly lit by shafts of bright sunlight which were shining through the circle of cumulous towering high above. The effect was strikingly dramatic, and very beautiful. But there was little time to enjoy the spectacle, because we had soon passed across it and had plunged once again into the violent, turbulent blackness of the storm clouds and the solid sheets of torrential rain.

This time, however, we passed through the trailing edge of the storm without too much difficulty, and we eventually emerged into the bright sunshine and calmer air at the fringe of the hurricane, much to everybody's relief.

As we cleared the last vestiges of cloud, the outline of the Andaman Islands showed up clearly on the horizon, just to the left of our track. The sight brought back vivid and uncomfortable memories of the scrap that we had had with the Japanese fighter just a few months before. But we had now reached the limit of our range. So, sadly, we turned for base, safely skirting the curtains of rain on the outskirts of the storm which by now had moved to the south of our track.

We eventually arrived back late at night with nothing to report to an anxious squadron, and with the uncomfortable knowledge that it would have been quite impossible to survive in a small rubber dinghy through the hurricane that we had just experienced, if indeed that was the area where they had gone down.

The search for 'X' was continued by us and other squadron aircraft for some time. But, eventually, it became obvious that there was no hope of finding the crew and passengers alive, and other squadron commitments were now becoming pressing. So, the search for 'X' was reluctantly abandoned, although the aircraft that were being used

to take ex-prisoners of war back to India were still briefed
to carry out a search during the transit. Every possible
attempt was made to locate the missing aircraft, but all
without success.

There was, however, a rather curious sequel to the tragic
story which, although easily and rationally explained, did
seem rather strange in the light of what had gone before.
Some weeks after the disappearance of 'X', when I was
carrying out the duty of Station Orderly Officer at Seletar, a
few British soldiers commanded by a warrant officer
arrived at the station, and requested accommodation and a
meal. When I enquired where they had arrived from and
where their unit was, it transpired that these extraordinarily
brave and modest men had been living and surviving in the
jungle ever since their regiment had been overcome by the
Japanese Army in the early part of the war; and despite the
inevitable hardships that they had undergone in the totally
alien environment of the jungle, they had not only survived
without being captured through all those long, terrible
years, but had also maintained their self discipline, and had
even been able to carry out a small number of limited
sabotage attacks against the enemy. They had apparently
survived mainly on vegetables and the game that they
obtained from the jungle; although they were also given
some very limited help by a few Malay villagers, who had
braved imprisonment or even death in order to help them.

After belatedly learning that the Far East war had finally
ended, they had decided to trek back to Singapore through
the jungle. On the way, they had spotted the wreckage of a
large aircraft, which was easily identified as British from the
rondels on its wings and sides. It was spread out over a wide
area across a hillside in Johore Bahru, only about thirty
miles from Singapore.

The wreckage was scattered over a wide area, and was
already becoming covered with thick, fast-growing jungle

plants, making a positive identification of aircraft type difficult for the non-expert. But the team sent out to identify and bury the dead quickly established that it was indeed the missing squadron flying-boat, and a number of photographs were taken of the crash site by the Warrant Officer in charge of the operation.

When he returned to Seletar, he approached me one evening in the mess with the photographs in his hand. But there was something odd and serious about his manner which immediately caught my attention. He silently handed me the shocking pictures of the crashed aircraft, one of which showed the indistinct but easily recognisable features of the aircraft's Flight Engineer in one corner. The photograph must, of course, have been a double exposure which had been taken at some time previously. But it did seem very odd to us at the time when I recalled the strange conversation that I had had with him on the night of the tragedy. There was a good deal of speculation among the now very subdued mess members that the Flight Engineer had had a premonition of his impending death. I, personally, dismissed the idea as too fanciful. Readers, however, must draw their own conclusions from the strange story.

What I now find difficult to understand is that it was only fifty years later, when I was writing the synopsis of this book and had thought more deeply about what had happened, that I realised the truth of what had actually occurred that night. The poor chap must have been suicidal, as it is the only way in which he could have possibly have known that they were going to crash into that hillside; and as a Flight Engineer he would have had sufficient technical knowledge and opportunity to cause the aircraft to crash. I now accept that with more understanding on my part, and by taking his place on the aircraft, I could have possibly saved the lives of nearly fifty people. The only comfort that I now have is that few people would have suspected an apparently well-balanced young man, who had faced the continuous dangers of operational flying over a long period without losing his nerve, would take the dreadful action that he did, with such tragic and awful consequences.

The initial success of the Japanese Army, in its ability to move rapidly over difficult jungle terrain and to spring the surprise attacks that it did in the early part of the war, was partly accounted for by the ability of the Japanese soldiers to live off the area through which they were travelling, usually by completely ignoring the needs of the local community and stealing any food that they could lay their hands on. They even took those stores, mainly of rice, that were necessary to prevent starvation of the local population. The theft of these reserves of food and the enforced neglect of the paddy fields during the war contributed to a shortage of food in Malaya, which had left many people on the verge of starvation.

Once again, the Sunderland flying-boats were pressed into service to perform a task that had never been envisaged for them, but which they were to perform outstandingly well. They delivered rice to the starving population of the port of Kuantan on the North Malayan coast.

Although we had pumped in only sufficient fuel to make the short transit to Kuantan and back, 'Zebra' was laying lower in the water than she ever had before, under a load of ten thousand pounds of rice stacked in sacks in her bomb bay, and she only responded sluggishly as we opened the throttles for take-off. But with the unrestricted sea room available to us in the Johore Straights, and a good chop on the water, she eventually came unstuck, and after a quick run up the North Malaysian coast we landed at the port of Quantan where the rice was unloaded by the local labourers almost before we had got the aircraft shut down and moored up. So desperate were the local people for food.

Our visit fortunately coincided with a parade at which captured Japanese Officers were to surrender their swords to the local British Commander, and we were invited to attend. The parade took place on a very large village green on which a wooden stage had been prepared for the ceremony, with seating arranged on it for all the local dignitaries.

When the prisoners were ordered on to the parade ground, a long line of Japanese Officers appeared, and quite deliberately and insolently slouched towards the saluting base, laughing and talking to each other as they did so. They were guarded, and dwarfed, by a contingent of the Indian Army.

The Officer commanding the parade was very obviously not going to stand for that sort of defiant behaviour from a defeated enemy, and ordered them off the parade ground in no uncertain terms to smarten themselves up and to show some respect to their captors. When they returned a second time, however, they were very much smarter. Marching up to the parade Commander, they saluted smartly, and correctly presented their swords to him with an obsequious bow. Their sudden change of heart was puzzling at first, until I noticed that the Indian troops had fixed bayonets during the interval, and from what I knew of the Indian soldiers, they were not the least adverse to applying the nice sharp tip of a bayonet to a Japanese posterior in a good cause. They had certainly made a deep impression upon the Japanese, who had quite obviously needed a sharp lesson in good manners.

One passenger decided to return with us to Singapore. He was the local doctor who had not seen his parents since the beginning of the war, and was naturally anxious for their safety. It was his intention to return to Kuantan on the next flight the following day, which was also loaded with rice. But if the good doctor had known what fate had in store for him, he might very well have changed his mind.

The following day 'T' left for Quantan, once again heavily loaded with rice for a normal quick run up the coast. But as the Fight Engineer explained to me afterwards, they made a normal approach and landing on the river, but as the aircraft sank into the water off the step at about sixty knots, there was a loud, frightening bang under the hull, and the aircraft shuddered as her bows dipped deeply into the river. This threw a sheet of obscuring water over the windscreen and into the inboard propellers. Almost immediately afterwards, water also surged up the companion way inside the aircraft leading to the flight deck, cutting off the intercom system and isolating the crew from one another.

The Captain, who was still unable to see through the partially obscured windscreen, immediately reacted by banging open the throttles and at the same time swinging the aircraft blindly round towards the river bank. He was just in time to beach the aircraft on the shelving mud flats that lined the tidal river before she sank.

Astonishingly, nobody on board was injured, apart from the odd small abrasion and bruise. The good doctor, however, had completely disappeared.

A few hours later, after a long search, he was discovered by the very worried crew, laying prostrate on a couch at home, and very much the worse for wear, having liberally laid into a bottle of the local arrack in order to calm his shattered nerves. I rather gained the impression from the condition of the crew when we met them the following day, that they had given the good doctor some considerable assistance with the bottle, after finding him so distraught.

Anyway, he turned out to be a very decent, hospitable chap, who invited all the crew home the following day, when we made the next run, to enjoy a special celebratory meal, which he had been saving up for years in order to celebrate the end of the war. It turned out to be a revolting, sticky gruel, which he and his family tucked into with the greatest relish. The crew, who were by now well used to the wholesome delights of wartime flying rations, faced the meal without flinching, and finished theirs up almost as though they had actually enjoyed it.

As the tide receded, it left 'T' high and dry on the mud flats, and her rice was quickly off loaded before it was destroyed. It was obvious then that she had hit some very large obstruction in the water, because a long section of the planing bottom of her hull had been ripped out. It was suggested locally that she probably hit a large salt water crocodile, which would have been partly submerged in the water making it difficult to see. But that was only supposition. Anyway, as she would no longer be of any use to us, I removed her plastic throttle knobs to replace the ones on 'Zebra' which had been so enjoyed by Ratty, and from then on we were able to enjoy the luxury of a complete set of throttles that had been so long denied to us by our old friend. He was, no doubt by now, thoroughly enjoying himself to the full in his adopted country Ceylon.

In between the frequent sorties there was time off to relax. The fine camp swimming pool, which had been used as a reservoir for oil by the Japanese, was quickly cleaned out and pressed back into service, and the local Tiger Beer, whose label bore a distinct resemblance to the squadron crest, but which had not been available to the squadron personnel for a long time, started to arrive in the messes, to everybody's complete satisfaction.

Life outside the city, in the kampongs, where the majority of the indigenous Malay people lived, was still very rural and easy-going, with the main source of transport being by oxen-drawn carts, and with most of the Malays relying on fishing and agriculture for their livelihood.

The Mandai was still a great swamp before it was eventually drained to become Seletar reservoir, now the main source of water for Singapore. When it was completed, it reduced the Singaporean's almost total dependence on Malaya for water, and Jurong, which is now highly industrialised and covered with factories, was in those days still covered with secondary jungle.

But the town was already bustling with life, because by this time thousands of servicemen from the three services were waiting in holding camps for ships to take them home to England and demobilisation. The night-life was accordingly stepped up to cater for them, and the result was pretty wild. In one case it also turned out to be tragic, because some of the drink available round the town had been laced with wood alcohol, which sent a number of Allied servicemen blind after drinking it. There was a rumour that the tampering had been carried out by the Japanese Army just before they surrendered, as a final desperate act. But it was much more likely to have been some smart businessman out to make a few extra dollars, whatever the eventual cost in human suffering.

Chapter Twelve

A Detachment to Labuan and Australia, and the Massacre of Japanese Prisoners of War

The next move for the crew of 'Zebra' was a detachment to Labuan, which is a small island off the north west coast of Borneo. We were tasked to take over the duties of an Australian Catalina flying-boat squadron who had been flying in food and supplies, and bringing out the wounded from the small native towns and villages dotted round the coast of Borneo, but who were now returning to Australia.

Living conditions were decidedly primitive in the tented camp which the Australians had bequeathed to us, with mud and water carrying everything in its path as it gushed in through the tents and underneath the campbeds during the nightly monsoon downpour.

Servicing facilities were non existent, so that when 'Zebra's' starboard float tensioning strut became loose, and required adjusting, the only way to get out to the float with a stable enough platform to work on, was to make up a raft, which we did by lashing together the trunks of some coconut trees that had originally been felled to make a clearing for the tented site in which we lived. We then supported it on some old, empty oil drums, although even that was not particularly steady. Anyhow, it did the job, after a fashion, although only after we had been unceremoniously deposited in the ocean on a few occasions, with the loss of a few bits and pieces that we had omitted to tie firmly round our waists.

We had been left a projector and a few films by the Australian crew from whom we had taken over. But our cinema was a sheet tied between two coconut trees and a few oil drums to sit on. Unfortunately, the south west monsoon was now upon us, so as soon as darkness fell and the show commenced, so would the rain. We would stick it out until the screen became impossible to see through the driving rain, and then head for the tents. In all the time that we spent in Labuan, I don't think that anybody ever saw the end of a film.

There was little to occupy one's time between the frequent flights, as the only small town on the island had been levelled by the fighting, with only the remains of a battered clock tower left standing, on which some wag had painted 'Labuan Town Hall'. There was, however, the pleasure of swimming in the warm breakers of the Indian Ocean, and, of course the cinema.

Although the only freshwater available to us came from a small stream, showering was no problem. All one had to do was to wait for the nightly outburst of torrential warm rain, and then stand out in it with a bar of soap. Hot water for shaving and washing clothes was, however, non existent.

Several ingenious methods were tried, by the inventors among us, to obtain hot water, which surprisingly to my mind did not result in death or serious injury to anyone. But that was more by luck than good judgement. The most efficient of these remarkable devices, was a can filled with one hundred octane aviation fuel which was tied to the trunk of a coconut tree. A small bore copper pipe led to the ground, where it was twisted roughly into a vertical spiral. It was intended to work like a blowtorch by its talented inventor. Unfortunately, and quite contrary to his expectations, it exploded violently at frequent intervals, and on one occasion set fire to a tent.

An alternative method was then tried, which this time consisted of an old oil drum with the top cut off, across which was placed a length of wood. The long metal blade of a screwdriver was pushed down into the water in the drum through a hole drilled in the wood. Then, when wires from the generator, which normally supplied electricity to the site, were connected to the screwdriver blade and the casing of the oil drum, the result was remarkable. The water boiled in seconds, much to everybody's delight. The effect on the clothing in the drum, however, was even more remarkable, because where it had contacted the metal blade of the screwdriver, large holes had been burnt in it. So, perhaps not too surprisingly, that device was also abandoned.

The squadron's task was to carry supplies, mail and the odd passenger to the isolated army units that were still situated in small towns and villages round the coast of Borneo, and to bring out any injured personnel requiring hospital treatment. This often meant landing and handling the aircraft on narrow rivers and creeks which would not have been contemplated under normal conditions. Both Pilots became very adept at manoeuvring the aircraft and gunning the outboard engines hard in order to swing the big boat round in the very confined spaces that were available to us.

Getting ashore was also quite often hazardous, as we relied on the local boatmen whose only transport, quite often, was dugout canoes, which were generally both unstable and unmanoeuvrable. This did not do much for 'Zebra's' paintwork, which was already looking decidedly battered anyway. Her sides quickly became scratched and scored by over enthusiastic native rowers. On one occasion, we all finished up in the river when our canoe overturned to the great delight of the villagers watching our progress on the bank. I was thankful, though, as I struggled, dripping wet, up the muddy river bank, that I had taken the trouble to learn to swim when I had been accepted for the Flight Engineers' course on flying-boats at St Athan.

On another flight to a remote village on the coast, we were given the dubious honour of being taken ashore in a beautifully carved and decorated ancient war canoe, which had been hewn out of the trunk of a giant jungle tree. It was called 'Watersnake', and in its prime was probably capable of carrying thirty or forty warriors with paddles. But the impressive effect of the massive and beautifully carved tree trunk was rather spoilt by the noisy outboard engine on the stern. The engine had been previously liberated from the Japanese by the villagers, although exactly how they had achieved that desirable result we were by now much too wise to ask.

We were solemnly assured, with much vigorous nodding of heads by the growing ring of half-naked warriors that had come to view the strangers who appeared to be about to invade their territory, that the canoe was no longer used for attacks on local villages, during which it had been customary to indulge in the pleasing pastime of cutting off all the defeated opponents' heads and parading them for everybody's edification on wooden bamboo spikes round the village.

But when regarding our hosts closely, I must say that I still entertained some doubts about their intentions, and was quite pleased when we were allowed to embark in one piece after being regarded with some malevolence by an old man from the dark interior of a Dyak long-house.

Although few of the local people could manage even a few words of English, and all conversation had to be conducted in sign language, which on their part seemed to mainly consist of waving their fearsome looking machetes and blow pipes about, there was however one short phrase known universally. That phrase was M and B 693. We later discovered, quite by accident I might hastily add, that this was the drug used to cure any affliction that had been caused by too close an association with ladies of the night.

By some strange stroke of extraordinary good fortune, none of the crew had had any previous experience or need of this particular remedy. It was only after some time, therefore, and a lot of rather odd gesticulating on the part of the little boys who would paddle alongside the aircraft as soon as the engines were shut down and the anchor had been dropped, that we realised what they meant. And we then found that the only way to get rid of them was to let them have the only surplus tablets left in our first aid kit.

Our next run took us to Jesselton to pick up a man who had been badly injured by an accident with a grenade. The river was really far too narrow for the operation of a big flying-boat, and the fast flowing current made manoeuvring difficult. But the Captain, with great skill, kept our out-board propellers clear of the overhanging jungle canopy as he swung 'Zebra' neatly round in a circle ready for the take-off run, and the wounded man was safely picked up and flown back for treatment to Cochin in Sarawak.

Cochin was a quiet and attractive little colonial town where we stayed on for a few days' relaxation in the relative comfort of a permanent army mess. But it was here in the gentle peace of Cochin that I was again to be quite inno-cently involved in a savage and brutal tragedy, which could not possibly have been foreseen, or indeed avoided, without prior warning.

The palace of Rajah Brooke, who was probably better known as the White Rajah, was just outside of Cochin. As the family were away from the town, we obtained permis-sion to pay it a visit. The palace was an unimpressive and large wooden building which we all found uninteresting, but just as I was leaving a young man, probably about thirty years of age, approached me and politely asked if I was a member of the crew of the flying-boat out on the river. He explained that he was the Rajah of Dutch Borneo. His elderly father had been forced to work down a mine by the Japanese. The unaccustomed hard work which he had been forced to do, coupled with very little to eat, and the normal ill-treatment meted out by the Japanese soldiers to their prisoners, had quickly killed the old man.

The Rajah had rounded up the Japanese Officers most probably responsible for the outrage, and wanted them flown back to Pontianak, in what was then Dutch Borneo, for identification, trial and sentencing. I introduced him to the Captain, who agreed to fly the prisoners thirty at a time, provided that they were well guarded on the flight and correctly treated as prisoners of war.

The next day, just before first light, as I waited on the jetty for the boat to take me out to 'Zebra' in the early morning, heavy, violent showers were blowing in shimmering waves across the blackness of the river, dotting the dark rushing, water with fountains of glistening spray; and in the distance, brilliant lightning flashes lit up the towering peaks of massed ranks of storm clouds that heralded the approach of a monsoon storm, and, almost drowning the noise of the flooding river, came the continuous growling rumbling of thunder which reverberated deafeningly across the jungle canopy.

Although, thankfully, I was unable to foresee it at the time, the tropical storm, in all its violent savage intensity, was a fitting and almost Wagnerian backdrop to the dreadful tragedy that was to take place later on that day.

The Japanese prisoners arrived accompanied by one Dutch soldier, who was only armed with a revolver. I hoped at the time that he was a jolly sight more proficient with a gun than I was, but he seemed confident enough.

His confident attitude was soon explained by the demeanour of the prisoners. They had obviously been completely cowered by the treatment that they had received at the hands of the Dutch soldiers. It was an attitude that contrasted sharply with the arrogant insolence displayed by the Japanese officers that we had seen on the surrender parade at Quantan. They had been treated correctly as prisoners of war by their British captors, but had tried to take every advantage of what they had interpreted as weakness.

The prisoners meekly sat down on the floor of the bomb bay when ordered to do so, and quietly remained there with their hands tied behind their backs, until we arrived at Pontianak just over an hour later.

We moored up to what looked remarkably like an empty oil drum, and probably was, which had previously been prepared for us close to a jetty. A long tree-lined avenue lead from the jetty into the centre of Pontianak. The long avenue was lined with well armed Dutch troops, which allayed any anxiety that we may have felt about the safety of the prisoners. But lining the river bank were some many hundreds of local people, all of whom were ominously heavily armed with machetes, knives, blowpipes and anything else that they could lay their hands on.

The crowd fell silent as the Japanese prisoners stepped into the dinghy, and remained so as they were ferried ashore. We watched them closely from the aircraft as they were escorted swiftly and safely down through the avenue of trees until they were out of our sight.

The uncanny silence, and the vicious hatred showing on the faces of the natives for the men who had inflicted such a terrible tyranny upon them, was frightening, and it certainly bode no good for the future of the prisoners. But for the time being at least they were safe. So, fairly reassured by what we had seen, we proceeded to shut down 'Zebra' and prepared to go ashore.

The intention of the Rajah had been to exhibit the Japanese officers in Bamboo cages which had been constructed in the middle of the town, with the hope that the men who had forced his father into a premature and awful death could be properly identified and then charged.

The local people, however, had other ideas about the prisoners' futures. As we were finally driven through the town square about half an hour later, on our way to the Dutch officers' mess, we saw that the bamboo cages had already been torn apart and violently strewn across the road, and that every prisoner had been hacked to death, with their bodies dismembered, and with their blood, which was still running in rivulets from the shattered cages, already turning black in the heat of the tropical sun.

Despite the quite deliberate reign of terror that the Japanese had inflicted on the local people in order to subdue them, it was still a harsh and dreadful retribution for the local people to take against unprotected prisoners of war, and one that we would have avoided at all costs if we could have possibly foreseen it. But it was difficult to totally condemn the perpetrators of the massacre, when remembering the atrocities that had been committed by Japanese soldiers that we had already both witnessed and heard about in Burma.

Although throughout the war years the crew of 'Zebra' had faced and witnessed many instances of violent death, and in some cases had actually contributed to it, the terrible sight that they witnessed that day had a profound effect upon them; and it was a very subdued and silent crew who flew back to Labuan the following day, vowing that the remaining sixty prisoners would remain properly protected and dealt with as prisoners of war.

Our best intentions, however, were defeated by an instruction from command to transport another thirty prisoners to Pontianak. This time, firm assurances had been given by the Dutch authorities that they would be properly treated and protected. But it was with very considerable misgivings that we found, when we arrived there, the same heavily armed mass of people lining the river bank that had been there on our previous visit.

The Dutch authorities were, however, as good as their word, and the prisoners were rapidly marched away to a secure compound. But I shuddered to think what would probably have happened to them after that, when remembering the intense and implacable hatred for the Japanese that we had encountered on our first visit.

As we prepared 'Zebra' for the return flight to Labuan, a dinghy pulled alongside the aircraft with a gift to the crew from the Rajah. It proved to be three large wicker baskets full of bottles of the locally brewed brandy. It tasted like, and had the creamy consistency of, a good quality yacht varnish. Nevertheless, it was very much appreciated by the squadron personnel when it was distributed round the detachment after we got back to Labuan. And a blissful few days ensued as a consequence.

With our task in Borneo nearly complete, the crew were looking forward to the return to Singapore, and eventually the journey back to the UK. But a problem had developed with the mass of American lease-lend arms and equipment, that by agreement with the Americans should have either been returned to the United States or destroyed when the war ended. Not surprisingly, perhaps, the equipment was disappearing at an alarming rate in the direction of Australia. So, a senior British officer was sent to visit various bases there to negotiate either its return or destruction, and we were the lucky crew detailed to fly him there.

Labuan island and the long coast line of Borneo were

still shrouded in what seemed to be the usual sheets of torrential driving rain and mist as we left it for the last time heading for Darwin, whose weather was disappointingly not very much better when we arrived. But our next stop at Cairns was much more interesting. In those days, Cairns was still a quiet little backwater, which reminded me, with its mainly dirt roads and wooden paths with hitching rails to tie up one's horse outside every building, of an American wild west frontier town film set.

Brisbane and Sydney came next, with little time for sightseeing. But a disaster of unprecedented proportions had struck the whole Australian nation at that time, because beer, which appeared to be the staple diet of every male over the age of ten, was in very short supply; and, as a terrible consequence, the pubs and bars were only open for one hour a day. The result of the shortage was that the scenes in Sydney's bars and pubs between the hours of five and six every evening were reminiscent of the worst battles of World War Two, as strong, thirsty Australian men fought for their only pint of the day. So, we were always forced to retire from the fray, heavily defeated and still thirsty.

By now, 'Zebra' was looking very much the worse for wear, with her once pristine white flanks streaked with oil and dirt, and her long shapely chines battered and dented by out of control bomb and refuelling scows, and roughly-hewn war canoes. The crew, who had attempted to smarten themselves up for the trip to Australia, were none the less still wearing the tattered khaki uniforms that it had been impossible to replace before we left Singapore. So it was a pretty rough looking bunch of brigands who arrived at Hobart in Tasmania, which was our next stop.

We made a couple of quick orbits around the harbour when we arrived, in order to assess the landing conditions, and were a little surprised to see a good deal of activity around the jetty.

When we arrived ashore, however, much to our astonished surprise and embarrassment, considering the state of our uniforms, we were met on the jetty by the Mayor of Hobart wearing all his finery, who in turn was followed by a whole host of dignitaries. They all proceeded to vigorously and solemnly shake our hands. There then followed a short silence, during which the Mayor and the Captain looked at each other in a puzzled sort of way. Eventually, however, the Mayor broke the uneasy silence and said, 'Well, where is it?' It was then just becoming clear to us that all was not quite what it had first seemed. However, the Captain, with engaging clarity said, 'Where's what?'

'The air mail, of course,' replied the Mayor uneasily.

So, the truth was finally out. Today was to be the inauguration of the resumed air mail service from the mainland to Tasmania, and we had arrived just prior to the first scheduled flight, and had been mistaken for it.

Nothing daunted the Mayor, who was distinctly a man of action and few words declared that he had flaming well waited long enough for the flaming air mail. So, without more ado, we were all invited to a reception that had already been laid on; and by the time the sparkling, polished scheduled flying-boat, that was actually carrying the mail, had landed and taxied in, the very smart crew were met by a solitary figure, who for the last hour had listened longingly to the rumpus emanating from the marquee, and who swiftly joined us before all the beer had disappeared. This left a slightly bemused crew to find their own way to the refreshment tent, where by this time they had some considerable difficulty in communicating with his worship, the Mayor.

I now find it difficult after the passage of all these years to remember quite what happened for the rest of that day; and I was later afflicted with much the same problem after an extended visit to a local Hobart brewery, which had been euphemistically described by the Captain as educational.

On the way back to Singapore, we once again taxied between the lines of gleaming white yachts into Sydney's Rose Bay, fully intending to spend at least one more night there. But with all the flying that we had carried out around Borneo, and the transit to Australia, Zebra's engines were now well past the scheduled time for a thorough overhaul. So, as a temporary measure that would get us back to base in one piece, and with the assistance of the whole crew, I cleaned the plugs and changed the engine oil.

The one hundred odd gallons of dirty black engine oil, however, had to be drained from underneath each engine nacelle, which meant balancing a couple of empty fifty gallon drums inside a small bouncing dinghy. Almost inevitably, just as the last few drops of oil dripped into the drum, we were hit by the wash of a local ferry. I lost my balance and tumbled into the water, closely followed by the oil. The crew dragged me on board looking like a jet black channel swimmer, and by the time I got cleaned up, all the lovely white yachts in the bay looked as though they had been repainted with black Plimsoll lines.

We all came to the unanimous decision at that point that it would be a very good time to leave the vicinity of Rose Bay. So, half an hour later, a dirty white flying-boat with a thick black line round its waterline could be seen streaking across the water of Sydney harbour on its rather guilty way to Brisbane.

We made a night stop to refuel at the island of Moratai on our way back to Singapore. It was a typical tropical island with the same lovely white beaches and graceful waving palm trees to which we had been accustomed. But the peace and quiet was shattered in the early morning by the ominous rattle of rifle fire at dawn.

It forcibly indicated to us that not all Allied servicemen

had the same respect for the rights of prisoners of war as we had, and that they often carried out their own brand of summary justice against a hated enemy.

Chapter Thirteen

The Final Transit Home

Singapore had become a much quieter place in our absence, as troop ships were now queuing in the harbour to take the troops home. But I was very shocked to learn that the majority of Royal Air Force ground crew in Singapore, Ceylon, India and Malaya had been on strike while we had been away, due to the slow arrival of troop ships to take them home.

There was some excuse for their frustration, because servicemen serving in the European theatre did not have to face the continuing dangers of the Far East war, which had continued for some time after Germany had capitulated; and they were also already being demobilised with the best of the civilian jobs available.

Despite the quite legitimate frustrations that they felt, I was, nevertheless, still surprised and shocked that the men who up until now had served their squadrons so faithfully and well, often in the most appalling and dangerous conditions, should suddenly behave with such apparent disloyalty.

The ring-leader of the strike in Singapore was eventually tried by court martial and sentenced to ten years in prison, although he eventually served only a small proportion of that sentence after being transferred to a prison in England.

A short period of inactivity followed our return from Australia, with only a few search and rescue operations to be carried out. But eventually the signal that we had all been waiting for arrived, and that was to fly the squadron back home to England.

We rocked our wings in a last sad salute to the crew and passengers of 'X', as we crossed the hill in Johore into which the aircraft had crashed that fateful night only a few months before, and then set a course which would take us straight across the centre of Sumatra on our way to Ceylon.

The sky was clear, with only some low patchy cloud and mist drifting off the jungle canopy as we coasted in; so, although the restricted altitude of the flying-boat meant that the short cut that we were taking would mean flying between the highest of the mountain peaks, it was decided that that would not be a problem with the visibility as good as it was.

With all the experience that we now had of the sudden unexpected and unpredictable changes of the tropical weather in the region, especially at the height of the monsoon, we should have known better. But as we started the steady climb up across the foothills of central Sumatra, the cloud began to thicken, and we were soon flying in eight eighths cloud, with the four twin Wasps beginning to labour with the increase in altitude.

My first indications that everything was not going quite according to plan, were the frequent and worried consultations between the Captain and the Navigator, and the nervous pacing up and down the flight deck. I looked questioningly at the Navigator as he passed me for the tenth time. He just pointed to his chart by way of an answer. Our track, which was shown as a thin black pencil line across his map, took us between two nine thousand foot mountain peaks which were only about five miles apart, and at that time we were flying at eight thousand feet and only gaining height slowly. It was a nail biting time as we waited to clear the cloud, expecting any moment to hit the hard centre of the mountains. Fortunately for us, it worked out all right in the end, because we finally broke through the dense cloud cover and slowly climbed into clear air, with the twin peaks thrusting their jagged heads out through the cloud just two or three miles behind us. We had flown cleanly between them in eight eighths cloud, with nothing but a magnetic compass and dead reckoning for navigation. Our journey home that day had very nearly come to an abrupt and permanent end, and that's for sure.

The mooring trots at Koggla were deserted as we banked overhead in preparation for landing there, because the squadrons which had originally operated out of there when we had first joined the squadron, a seeming lifetime away, had either returned to England or were staying on in Singapore; and the mess that had witnessed the wild celebrations of VJ night was now deserted and quiet.

I set off after dinner in a rickety taxi to visit my old friends, One Leg and his First Mate. The village was just as I had remembered it during my first visit in the early dawn, with the flickering light from the log cooking fires casting a warm glow over the plaited coconut fronds that covered the roofs of the basha huts.

The whole village remembered me as the simpleton who thought that he was just going out for a relaxing day's fishing in the lagoon. But with the greatest kindness and courtesy, and a lot of laughing and shouting, they all accompanied me down to the beach, where One Leg and his First Mate were repairing their nets, and still exercising their quite extraordinary skills with copious mouthfuls of betal nut juice. I spent a pleasant hour reminiscing with my two friends, and was sorry to leave them and the gentle, friendly peace of the village when I had to finally return to camp.

We left Koggala, taking great care to avoid the little island in the middle of the flare path, and then flew up the west coast of India to Karachi, where we spent the night, and then on across the Arabian sea to Habaniya, in Iraq.

The next stop was Cairo, where we landed on the Nile and were accommodated in one of the original paddle steamers, that had been used for the passengers and crews by the old Imperial Airways flying-boats before the war. The quiet peaceful luxury that we enjoyed there was a very far cry from the anxiety, noise and steamy heat of Burma.

The unrest that eventually gave Egypt its independence was already beginning to manifest itself there, as it was all over the Far and Middle East. As a result, our coach was stoned by gangs of Egyptian youths as we passed through the outskirts of Cairo. So, despite the unaccustomed luxury and comfort that we had enjoyed there, we were glad to leave Egypt early the following morning to continue our journey home, which from then on was uneventful. Well, the flying was. Eventually, however, I saw down through gaps in the drifting cloud, the small bright green fields of England, and then felt the familiar jerk as our keel lightly kissed the waters of Pembroke Dock. We settled gently down into the water, taxied in and moored up. We were home at long last.

After a short and riotous disembarkation leave, we flew 'Zebra' up to London and landed her on Greenwich Reach, where the old girl proved to be a very popular attraction. Londoners had already personally experienced, and knew more about, the dangers of war from the German blitz, than most people, and were, therefore, fascinated by the sight of an operational aircraft that still bore the visible marks of her active service on the other side of the world.

That sortie was to be the last time that we were to fly 'Zebra'. She was still streaked with oil and dirt, and still bore the scars and dents from the endless encounters that she had had with floating tree trunks and unwieldy refuelling scows on many tropical lakes and rivers on the other side of the world. Her paintwork was scored and scratched from when we had flown her at low level, for many long hours, through the violence of the monsoon storms. But she was still riding high in the water, as though proud of the part that she had played with us all in the bitter savage turmoil of the Burma war.

We had used her awesome power to the full, and the men who had flown with her had faced danger and hardship steadfastly, and without flinching. So it was a sad, but very proud, man who turned away and left her for the last time.